UNCERTAIN PERIL

Uncertain Peril

Genetic Engineering and the Future of Seeds

Claire Hope Cummings

BEACON PRESS, BOSTON

Beacon Press
25 Beacon Street
Boston, Massachusetts 02108-2892
www.beacon.org

Beacon Press books
are published under the auspices of
the Unitarian Universalist Association of Congregations.

10 09 08 07   8 7 6 5 4 3 2 1

This book is printed on acid-free paper that meets the uncoated paper
ANSI/NISO specifications for permanence as revised in 1992.

Text design and composition by Tag Savage
at Wilsted & Taylor Publishing Services

Illustration by Alison Kendall

Portions of this work appeared previously
in *World Watch Magazine* in a different form.

"A Cabinet of Seeds Displayed" by Howard Nemerov is
reprinted herein by permission of Margaret Nemerov.

Library of Congress Cataloging-in-Publication Data

Cummings, Claire Hope
Uncertain peril : genetic engineering and the future of seeds /
Claire Hope Cummings.
p. cm.
Includes index.
ISBN 978-0-8070-8580-6
1. Agricultural biotechnology—Political aspects. 2. Transgenic plants—
Economic aspects. 3. Transgenic plants—Risk assessment. 4. Consumer
protection—Citizen participation. 5. Seeds—Biotechnology. I. Title.

S494.5.B563C86 2008
631.5'21—dc22   2007026298

For Richard,
the love of my life

For we have forgotten this: that the Earth is a star of grass,
a seed-planet, swirling with spores as with clouds, from sea to sea,
a whirl of them. Seeds take hold under the cobblestones
and between the letters in my poem, here they are.

from "Green Light," by Rolf Jacobsen,
translated from the Norwegian by Roger Greenwald

CONTENTS

A Green Wealth

A NOTE ON THE TERMINOLOGY

I use the words "biotechnology" and "genetic engineering" interchangeably, along with references to transgenics and to GMOs, or "genetically modified organisms." In all cases I am referring to recombinant DNA technology, as it is used to breed new organisms by crossing species boundaries. I am not using the term "biotechnology" in its general sense, which can include natural processes.

This analysis focuses exclusively on genetic engineering as it is used in agriculture. Genetic engineering has many other applications, particularly in medicine. Some of the arguments made here may apply to those uses, but only coincidentally.

Last, sometimes I refer to plants and seeds as if they were the same, which of course they are not. In some cases, where I was unable to make a finer point, I resorted to generalizations. Some of these generalizations will rankle experts, and for that I apologize in advance.

PREFACE

Yet, in holding scientific research and discovery in respect, as we should, we must be alert to the equal and opposite danger that public policy could itself become the captive of a scientific-technological elite.

PRESIDENT DWIGHT D. EISENHOWER, *1961*

Wheeler Hall, University of California, Berkeley

The audience was growing restive. Inside the darkened auditorium were some of the world's most eminent scientists, biotechnology's wealthiest entrepreneurs, the press, and invited guests. It was March 1999, and they had gathered to celebrate the first twenty-five years of biotechnology. The keynote speaker was the famous James D. Watson, who, along with Francis Crick, first described the double-helix structure of DNA.

Everyone wanted to hear Watson's reminiscences about the early years of molecular biology, but he was having problems getting started. He spent the first ten minutes of his speech trying to get a slide to focus. He kept ordering the technicians around and making lame jokes about Berkeley being a liberal arts school. Watson, who was then in his early seventies, began getting peevish.

Finally he moved on. But for the rest of the time he spoke, he had worked up a lather in his mouth that made him sound like he was speaking underwater. He kept making breathy gurgling noises into the microphone and nervously laughing at his own jokes. His speech turned into a rambling collection of fascinating details about how scientific discoveries are made, mixed in with gratuitous swipes at prominent colleagues. He told stories about personalities and academic infighting and threw in strange asides about women's bodies and "left-wing loonies." He said, "We are immensely better off because we didn't listen to the Friends of the Earth, the Sierra Club, all these people who just wanted us to prove what we were doing was safe before we do it."

The remarkable thing about Watson's speech that day was not so much that his quirky personality was on display; it was what he said about the role of science in society. The telling moment came as he was recalling the first recombinant DNA experiments. At the time, scientists were using tumor viruses and *E. coli* bacteria to cut genetic material from one organism and insert it into another. Watson acknowledged that early on, scientists had concerns about the safety of those experiments. He said they all felt that Nobel laureate Joshua Lederberg had it right when he said genetic engineering held both "certain promise and uncertain peril." Now, however, Watson was unequivocal. He said that this technology held such "certain promise" that it should not be constrained by fears of "uncertain peril."

Watson expressed his disdain for the controversy this technology was causing and urged his colleagues to disregard the critics. Instead of explaining why he chose "certain promise" over "uncertain peril," he mocked concerns about this technology and the people who expressed them. In some ways, he was simply saying out loud what many in the audience already thought. Watson was also defending his own role in promoting the development of recombinant DNA technology and his antipathy toward public debate. Although he didn't dwell on the part he played in marginalizing the public, he was there when the decisions were made.

In 1973, just as recombinant DNA technology was beginning to be developed, the scientific community met to discuss safety concerns at the Asilomar Conference Center in Pacific Grove, California. They wanted to discuss, in private, a way to develop a system of voluntary controls that would leave scientists in charge of oversight. Then, in February 1975, a larger and more public meeting was held at Asilomar. By then, serious safety issues were emerging, including the possibility of uncontrolled experiments, mutant viruses, new pathogens, and threats to human health. It was a rare collective discussion by scientists involved in a new technology, but it was by no means open-ended. Those who attended were not so much concerned with public safety as they were determined to forestall a larger, potentially more acrimonious public debate over the risks of genetic engineering.

According to science historian Susan Wright, the assembled scientists decided they would be self-regulating. They believed that they could come up with technological fixes for any problems that might arise, and they preserved for themselves the exclusive right to define, regulate, and benefit from genetic engineering. There was, according to Wright, virtual unanimity for this idea. She said it bore "within it the seeds of a technical solution expressed in personal and economic interests."

These decisions created a central role for the research community in policymaking, to the exclusion of society in general. From then on, Wright says, this "reductionist discourse" became dogma and eventually defined the boundaries of the public's role in genetic engineering. As a result of this one remarkable meeting, which occurred long before the products of genetic engineering were commercialized, there has never been a public debate about the risks and benefits of this revolutionary new technology.

Watson's speech at Berkeley ended with the enthusiastic applause of his colleagues. For his part, Watson was not simply betraying his own cynicism about the role of the public; he was revealing a much deeper animus that underlies genetic engineering and all its progeny: the age-old idea that mankind is entitled to control the natural world. And it reveals a more subtle foe: the danger to our democracy that comes from any diminution of the public discourse. The right to choose what we eat and to know what is in our food is a fundamental human freedom. But the decisions made at Asilomar by men like Watson undermined the role of the public and our government in securing our environmental health and public safety. Agricultural biotechnology was commercialized without regard to these important citizen and consumer rights.

This is the soft tyranny of the technological elite. James Madison, the fourth president of the United States, warned us that our liberty was at stake when we no longer participated in decisions about something as fundamental as what we eat when he said "a popular government, without popular information or the means to acquire it, is a prologue to a farce, or a tragedy, or perhaps both." It is most definitely the path of uncertain peril.

INTRODUCTION

Spitsbergen Island, Svalbard, Norway

On a frozen island near the North Pole, a huge hole has been blasted out of the side of an Arctic mountain and a tunnel has been drilled deep into the rock. When the facility under construction here is completed, it will be lined with one-meter-thick concrete, fitted with two high-security blast-proof airlock doors, and built to withstand nuclear war, global warming, terrorism, and the collapse of the earth's energy supplies. It's known as the "Doomsday Vault," and in it will be stored millions of seeds and mankind's hope for the future of the world's food supply.

The idea is that in the event of massive ecological destruction, those seeds could be used to reconstruct the planet's agricultural systems. Exactly who might remain to begin replanting the earth after such a catastrophe is only one of the questions this astounding project raises. The more immediate question is, are seeds in peril? The answer is yes, especially the seeds that provide us with food, fiber, and fuel. Both the diversity and the integrity of seeds are threatened, in the wild and on our farms. They are being put at risk by agricultural technologies, patents and corporate ownership, and the overall degradation of the environment. The plight of seeds is one of the most important environmental stories of our time. Until now, however, this critical issue has not received the attention it deserves.

Seeds are as critical to our survival as air, water, and soil. And yet despite the everyday miracles that they perform, we tend to take them for granted. Seeds sustain the beauty and vitality of the earth. Seeds are essential to the regenerative capacity of the planet. We will need their natural resilience and adaptability even more as temperatures rise. Biologically, each seed has a unique way of fulfilling its promise. Taken together, the world's seeds maintain the plant systems that keep the planet breathing. Every breath we take has been exhaled by a plant which turned it into oxygen for us. Seeds have always been our silent partners in maintaining life on earth.

People and plants coevolved through the ages, and that relationship has been mutually beneficial. Seed plants dependably meet our needs, producing the corn and rice we eat, the flax and cotton we weave, and the oak and pine we use for shelter. Eighty percent of the people in the world still rely on plants as their primary source of medicine. The remains of long-dead plants provide all of us with our fossil fuels. As metaphors, seeds are a rich source of inspiration in art, literature, and religion. We cannot afford to lose any more of this generosity, this beauty, this abundance.

We find ourselves at a dramatic turning point for life on earth. Population and consumption are rapidly expanding. Industrial food production is exhausting the planet's basic biological support systems, making them even more vulnerable to the effects of global warming. The natural world is experiencing catastrophic losses of biodiversity, fresh water, and fertile soil. All of these trends are threatening seeds and forcing us to take a careful look at how we will feed ourselves in the future. It comes down to this: whoever controls the future of seeds controls the future of life on earth.

Is industrial agriculture, with its focus on chemical and genetic technologies, the best choice for ensuring a healthy future? Genetic engineering is a commercial technology controlled by private corporations, who use it to dominate agricultural production from seed to stomach and to profit from every bite.

Given the enormous environmental stress the planet is under right now and increasing demands on our natural resources from all forms of human activity, can this one technology provide for our food and environmental security? The answer is, unequivocally, no.

There are five solid reasons that genetic engineering is not right for agriculture. One: it's bad science. It was developed on the basis of flawed assumptions which have since been discredited by the scientific community. Two: it's bad biology. It was deployed without regard for its potential for genetic contamination and its risks to human health. Three: it's bad social policy. It puts control over seeds and the fundamentals of our food and farms into the hands of a few corporations who have their own, not our, best interests in mind. Four: it's bad economics. After billions of dollars and thirty years, only a few products have been commercialized, and they offer nothing new. No one asked for genetically modified organisms (GMOs), and given a choice, consumers would reject them. Five: it's bad farming. GMOs don't address the real issues plaguing agriculture; they're designed to substitute for or increase the use of proprietary weed and pest control chemicals. Patented and genetically altered seeds perpetuate the very worst problems of the industrial food system, and they are undermining the autonomy of the farmers who use them.

According to the Global Crop Diversity Trust, the organization that is building the Doomsday Vault, there are more than 50,000 edible plants in the world. About 150 of them have been commercialized, and only 40 of those are cultivated regularly. Only three of them—rice, corn, and wheat—provide most of humanity with its mainstay foods. Three others—soy, cotton, and canola—get more than their fair share of attention because of their industrial uses. Other plants are important sources of sustenance for many people in the world, especially potatoes, cassava, and taro, as well as barley and sorghum. That's the short list of plants that we rely on for our basic needs, and all of them, as well as tobacco, sugar, coffee, sunflowers, and most fruits and vegetables, have been patented or genetically modified.

Seeds are the common heritage of all humanity, and yet they are being stolen right from underneath our noses. If someone came into your kitchen and took all the food off the shelves and out of the refrigerator, you'd notice. If someone came onto your farm and stole the seeds you were about to plant, you'd notice. But the theft of the world's genetic heritage has not been so overt. It's been done by changing the biological and legal character of plants, so that while the food and seeds remain where they were, ownership of them has shifted.

While all this has been going on, there have been plenty of welcome countertrends. A dynamic new food and farming movement is rising up all over the world, bringing local food and farming back to life and restoring agriculture to its ecological roots. This is where the hope lies. It can be found in the natural world, in the promise of the seed, and in the hands of the farmers and the native planters who tend the earth with the wealth of nature in mind. Organic farmers, chefs, urban and rural youth, artists, and activists are all working in their own ways, and sometimes together, to change the way we produce and consume food. New sustainable strategies and green technologies are being created. There are many proven ways to produce food and energy that protect both human health and the life of our soil and water while providing for our prosperity. These new agrarians are restoring respect for the skills of the human hand and the ingenuity of the natural world. They're putting the culture back into agriculture.

The story of agriculture is often told as the story of man's domination of nature. Now a new story is being told. The new story of agriculture combines the guidance of the old creation myths with the insights of science. We are learning the language of generosity from nature and of tolerance from our experiences in returning to local economies. As we go about searching for ways to return meaning and morality to our lives, and possibly, dare I hope, to the political system, the decisions we make now, and the wisdom that we choose to guide us, will make all the difference. What's at stake is nothing less than the nature of the future.

The Doomsday Vault is only one way of preparing for an uncertain future. Someday we may be glad it was built. My hope is that we will create a future for ourselves in which it will never be needed. Right now we can let others decide our fate and continue living in a fundamentalist "Frankenstate" where the corporate gene giants feed us artificial food and drugs produced with their genetically modified patented plants and lull us into complacency with their choice of electronic conveniences and entertainment. Or we can summon the courage to resist the worst of all that and begin restoring ourselves to our rightful places, as members of both human and biological communities and caretakers of our commonwealth.

We are facing a planetary emergency, as Al Gore says, but our "collective nervous system" still has trouble recognizing the threats to our survival. As an environmental journalist, I see this all the time. I often feel it myself. I wrote this book because I love seeds and because I have found that telling the stories of the people and places behind these issues can help us face them and the complex challenges they present. Industry spends millions telling its story and defending its products, and it stands poised to convert our upcoming ecological crisis into a commercial opportunity. I'm not offering a prescription for the future, just an invitation to consider our options carefully. The answers we need will come when we begin the conversation that starts with telling and listening to each other's stories.

I have brought all my life experiences, as a mother, a farmer, an environmental lawyer, an advocate for traditional native land rights, and a journalist, to weave together a meaningful context for the subject of genetic engineering and the future of seeds. All of my work has been guided by one central value: respect for the integrity of the natural world. This is what I have learned: if we can, even for a moment, pause and stop looking at the world through the lens of technology, then suddenly the beauty and wonder of nature reappear. Then we remember who we are and where we are, and the healing begins.

The Rise of the Techno-elites

ONE

Trade Secrets

History celebrates the battle-fields whereon we meet
our death, but scorns to speak of the ploughed fields
whereby we thrive; it knows the names of the king's
bastards, but cannot tell the origin of wheat. That is
the way of human folly.

J. H. FABRE, *The Wonders of Instinct*

Abu Ghraib, Baghdad, Iraq

Iraq is located in the legendary Fertile Crescent of the Middle
East, where wheat, barley, lentils, and other important grains
were first domesticated thousands of years ago. Ancient texts, the
Bible, archaeological evidence, and LANDSAT images have led
scholars to believe that southern Iraq might be where the biblical Garden of Eden was. An ancient valley, now underwater, has
been found where the Tigris and Euphrates Rivers, mentioned in
the Book of Genesis, empty into the Persian Gulf.

Iraq has a priceless seed heritage. Since ancient times, cereals,
vegetables, dates, fiber, and medicinal plants that are unique to
Iraq have been grown here. In the mid-1970s, Iraq's Ministry of
Agriculture gathered seeds from all over the country and established a collection containing 1,400 different "accessions," or distinct varieties. They built a seed bank along with a plant-breeding
institute and botanical garden in a suburb west of Baghdad known
as Abu Ghraib, not far from the now infamous prison. Then, in

March 2003, in the chaos surrounding the invasion of Baghdad by U.S. troops, Iraq's seed bank was destroyed.

Two months later, in May 2003, L. Paul Bremer, a Harvard MBA, was given the job of restoring Iraq's infrastructure. Along with his Brooks Brothers suits and work boots, Bremer brought with him the neoconservative values he shared with his boss, then secretary of defense Donald Rumsfeld. Bremer spent thirteen months and over $12 billion in cash ($9 billion of which has never been accounted for) and issued one hundred orders designed to create a market economy, including the agricultural sector, tailored to American interests. According to the UN Food and Agriculture Organization (FAO), before the invasion, 97 percent of Iraqi farmers saved seed from their own crops or bought it in their local markets. Although years of war and sanctions had already weakened their capacity to provide for themselves, the invasion and occupation not only ruined Iraq's own seed industry, it made Iraqi farmers dependent on U.S. aid.

Just before he left in April 2004, Bremer issued Order Number 81, a law that was aimed at the heart of Iraqi seed saving and caused an international outcry. Originally it was thought to be an outright ban on seed saving by Iraqi farmers, but it did not go that far. It did, however, effectively replace the practice of local seed saving by placing control over seeds in the hands of the Ministry of Agriculture and creating the legal mechanisms for the use of patented and genetically engineered seeds.

After Order 81 was issued, an international group of scientists wrote to Iraq's minister of agriculture at the time, Dr. Al-Sharifi, warning her that patented seeds could seriously damage her country's agriculture. One report in 2005 discussed the possible introduction of transgenic wheat into Iraq, but there is no evidence that this has been done. The U.S. Department of Agriculture (USDA), which is in charge of agricultural reconstruction, will not reveal the sources of its seed aid. The Defense Department delivers "foundation" wheat seed, source unknown, to farmers in unmarked bags. Transgenic wheat is not being grown commercially in the United States because U.S. and Canadian farmers have rejected it. But Monsanto and other companies are looking for places to get it established. What is clear is that the United States intends to use the occupation as an opportunity to remold Iraqi agriculture to fit American agribusiness interests. The USDA appointed Dan Amstutz, a former executive of Cargill, one of the world's largest grain-trading companies, to oversee agricultural reconstruction. As Thoreau said, "Some circumstantial evidence is very strong, as when you find a trout in the milk."

The USDA could be helping Iraqi farmers reestablish their domestic crops and seed independence. But that kind of open generosity has long been missing from our foreign aid policies. U.S. aid does not go to farmers; it is used to pay American corporations to dump their surplus commodities on the poor. Aid programs are often used to pressure third world farmers to adopt industrial agriculture and farm for the global grain trade. If they are too poor to farm, they are given food aid, often in the form of genetically modified organisms, or GMOs. In 2002, the only whole-grain food aid available from the United States was transgenic corn. That year, African countries where people were suffering from famine were told they had to accept GMOs, over the protests of countries like Zambia, which said the GMOs would contaminate their local corn seed, reduce crop yields, and make it difficult for their farmers to export to Europe.

Throughout the third world, traditional farmers act as the guardians of the world's most important crops and their genetic diversity when they save and breed their own seed. When our aid policies impose patented and genetically altered seeds on other countries, they deepen the suffering of the world's poor by increasing their dependency and taking away their seed sovereignty. By depriving them of the foundation of their economic independence and the resilience of their locally adapted crops, our aid policies actually subsidize poverty and hunger. And by replacing traditional seeds with modern commercial varieties, we contribute to the destruction of the world's seed diversity. As a result, third world farmers, and ultimately our own agricultural systems, are even more vulnerable than before to the effects of war, poverty, and environmental degradation.

The importance of traditional farming and seed saving has been validated by the largest consortium of seed banks in the world, the Consultative Group on International Agricultural Research (CGIAR). A CGIAR study of forty-seven countries affected by war and natural disasters concluded that the small farmer/seed holder was the key to successful reconstruction efforts. Local seed saving, says CGIAR, rebuilds local food systems, safeguards biodiversity, and helps reestablish food security. It says that integrating seed independence into aid programs enhances their effectiveness.

Our reconstruction efforts in Iraq could have created a real "green zone"—a secure area for agriculture to flourish, where traditional farming and seed diversity could thrive. In the context of postwar reconstruction efforts, neglecting local seed-saving strategies is simply irresponsible. But it's not surprising. The way the USDA and its allies in agribusiness are treating third world farmers is not that much different from the way they treat U.S. farmers.

The Reconstruction of American Agriculture

At the start of the twentieth century, American farmers were the most productive producers of food and fiber in the world. They fed their families, contributed to the larger food economy, and maintained their self-sufficiency by saving their own seeds. Their efforts were supported by a well-respected system of public plant research. By the end of the twentieth century, most American farmers had become dependent on the "domestic aid" of government subsidies and a handful of agribusiness corporations to provide them with patented seeds and the chemicals that go with them. Agribusiness's long-term strategy has been to eliminate the autonomy of farmers as independent producers.

If we were talking about widgets it might not matter, but farming is different. Farming provides a nation with more than its nutrition. It provides social stability, environmental integrity, and historical continuity. And farming is a major factor in our public health. Farming is also what keeps our most useful crops flourishing. In *Shattering: Food Politics and the Loss of Genetic Diversity*, Cary Fowler and Pat Mooney point out that with "people of the world from Boston to Bangkok dependent on thirty kinds of plants for the bulk of their sustenance, one does not have to be a nature-lover to be concerned about the extinction of traditional crop varieties and their wild relatives." One of the most important functions of agriculture is the preservation of useful crops and the integrity of seeds.

In the twentieth century, the balance between plant development and preservation shifted and the focus of agriculture became more utilitarian and oriented to commercial varieties. This trend was accelerated by the commercialization of hybrid seeds. Hybrids are created when two parents from different varieties are combined. Their first offspring can be more productive and reliable, but they do not produce seed that is true to type, so they have to be re-created from the original parents every year. That turned out to be a real boon to the seed business. Initially farmers had to be talked into using hybrid seeds, especially corn. Previously, seeds had been available for free or were easy to reproduce and exchange. Now they had become a commodity.

Then, after World War II, the chemicals that had been used as explosives, defoliants, and nerve gases were converted into fertilizers, herbicides, and pesticides. Like hybrid seeds, these products too were aggressively promoted. Farmers were told that this was the new, "scientific" way to farm. Agrochemical companies like Dow, DuPont, and Monsanto grew rich and politically powerful. Farmers were persuaded to abandon their "old-fashioned" methods of ensuring soil fertility and effective weed and pest controls and get on the chemical bandwagon.

Chemicals and improved "modern" varieties of seeds increased production, but that in turn caused prices to bottom out, and farms began to fail. The size of farms increased as the survivors bought out their neighbors. Farm income for these larger,

more industrial, commodity farms became increasingly dependent on government subsidies. By the 1970s, American farmers
had descended into a state of permanent economic crisis and the
diversified family farm was quickly disappearing as a mainstay of
American life. Once farmers were firmly established on the technology treadmill, it was a simple matter to get them to adopt the
next new thing: genetically engineered seeds.

The addiction analogy applies. As farmers became chemically
dependent, they constantly had to increase productivity and use
bigger and fancier machines and more land, water, and chemicals in order to keep up with each other and qualify for their
subsidies. Inevitably, the synthetic fertilizers and pesticides they
depended on began to lose their effectiveness. New and stronger
chemicals were needed. Some chemicals, like DDT, were banned.
The agrochemical industry knew that its mainstay chemicals
would eventually have to be replaced, and it found its salvation in
genetically engineered seeds.

GMOs were not invented because farmers were asking for
them. They were created as part of a larger business strategy to
gain and maintain control over the agricultural sector. For most
of the twentieth century, farmers relied on public research institutions and extension agents for advice and improved plant varieties. But biotechnology bypassed the existing public system.
This radical new product—a plant designed to use more chemicals—was created by industry, for industry. It sprang full-blown
as a finished product from the industry's laboratories, and the industry used its expertise in marketing and political manipulation
to commercialize the newfangled seeds.

The Birth of Biotechnology

The history of biotechnology is not well known. It comes as a
surprise to most people to find out that it was not a scientific
discovery. Genetic engineering technology was deliberately de-
vised by a small group of people who were looking for a way to

manipulate life according to their own designs and for their own purposes. Once they identified genes as a material basis for life, they figured out how to manipulate them, using recombinant DNA technology, and they immediately found commercial uses for their products.

The underlying conceit is what MIT science historian Lily Kay calls the "molecular vision of life." It came about, she says, as the result of the effort of a few scientists, along with their academic and philanthropic sponsors, who had a shared vision about how they could use genes to reshape science and society. Kay says this small group of people laid claim to DNA as a means to an end, once they decided that it was "the secret of life."

This new "protein paradigm" reduced the enormous complexity of life down to a few component parts and provided a biological basis for the idea that microorganisms could be engineered. This was the "new biology." It was seen as a mandate to take active control of life and was considered an improvement over the "old biology," which was a more passive observation and study of life. Molecular biology dominated science, and the public imagination, in the latter half of the twentieth century, a time when engineering feats fed most of our dreams for progress.

Kay explains that this new molecular view of the world fit in with other social values that were emerging at the time. There was, says Kay, a strong belief on the part of those involved in the importance of "industrial capitalism" and its perceived mandate for "science-based social intervention." Not everyone involved was in on some grand conspiracy. The work of many disinterested and well-intentioned scientists played a part. Nevertheless, genetic engineering came about because a select group of people worked together to further their mutual self-interests. It was the result of an intentional strategy, one that was clearly understood from the outset to be a useful tool for both social and biological engineering. And it offered those who adopted it a previously unimagined mastery over both nature and society.

The idea that a few people with special knowledge can solve

the world's problems gained traction in the early twentieth century. The field of sociology was beginning to become popular, and it supported the idea that intractable social problems were amenable to "salvation through experts." Genetics was also capturing the popular imagination. The idea that genes might be used to solve social problems gathered momentum in the 1930s and was given impetus by the development of technocratic forms of social control, particularly in Nazi Germany. Eugenics was fashionable in the United States too. While the science of genetics had not developed much beyond the basic principles of heredity outlined by Mendel in the nineteenth century, the 1930s was a time when the idea that genes determined traits gained traction.

The eugenic notion that there were "good" genes and "bad" genes, and good and bad traits, and the seductive thought that we actually had a choice between them, began to take hold. In 1928, George Bernard Shaw made fun of the idea that we could know what's best in this regard. In an essay on eugenics, he said, "Considering that we poisoned Socrates, crucified Christ, and burnt Joan of Arc amid popular applause, because, after a trial by responsible lawyers and churchmen, we decided that they were too wicked to be allowed to live, we can hardly set up to be judges of goodness or to have any sincere liking for it." Eugenics still permeates decisions made in animal breeding, both for use in agriculture and for our domestic pets.

The search for a science-based social agenda soon found favor, and funding, from both business and philanthropy. Inevitably, as the combined efforts of the public and private sectors bore fruit, the private sector became more involved. The desire for patents and profits sweetened the prospects for all concerned. Kay says the long-standing boundaries between what was "public" and what was "private" were erased as corporate and government interests merged. At the same time, the public role was being intentionally shunned, especially in the area of plant breeding. What emerged was a matrix of control. Biotechnology began to dominate scientific research, first by providing a way to take biological control over the organism itself and then by reengineering the regulatory system to suit its needs. Then the biotechnology industry took control of the marketplace and of public opinion through the use of "perception management" techniques.

In the end, it's been the triumph of what Kay calls the "technocratic approach to life." Inevitably, she says, with "the rise of quasi-public entities such as large business corporations and foundations," the boundary between individual and corporate self-interest, between private and public control, "would be increasingly blurred." The vision of the techno-elites was nothing less than the utopian desire, as Kay writes, to use "the expertise of the human sciences to stem what was perceived as the nation's social and biological decay and [to] help realize the vision of America's destiny."

Whether it was intended or not, the way biotechnology was developed has resulted in a relatively small number of players achieving an unprecedented and overarching level of control over life on earth. It brings to mind the words of Justice William O. Douglas, who warned that "as nightfall does not come at once, neither does oppression. In both instances, there's a twilight where everything remains seemingly unchanged, and it is in such twilight that we must be aware of change in the air, however slight, lest we become unwitting victims of the darkness."

Kay published her history of molecular biology in 1993, before the first agricultural products were released. By 2003, GMOs not only dominated commodity agriculture in America, they had infiltrated our foreign policy and food aid. In 2002, Secretary of State Colin Powell defended U.S. efforts to impose GMOs on the third world during the closing session of the United Nations Summit on Sustainable Development in South Africa. He was jeered. But his successors continue their efforts to impose agribusiness interests and their private technologies on Zimbabwe and Iraq, and wherever farmers lack the ability to resist, including America.

There Oughtta Be a Law

The dismantling of the U.S. regulatory system was a key element in the agrochemical industry's successful strategy to impose GMOs on the marketplace. Much of the controversy surrounding genetically engineered plants can be attributed to the fact that they are not effectively regulated and the public has no way of knowing whether or not they are safe. Agrobiotechnology has been commercialized by companies like Dow, DuPont, Syngenta, and Monsanto, all of which have a long history in the chemical business and a lot of experience avoiding government regulation. In *Trade Secrets,* a scathing exposé of the chemical industry televised on PBS, Bill Moyers shows how these companies knew as early as the late 1950s that their products were toxic. But these companies were concerned not with public health but with avoiding responsibility for the harm they caused. Then, because of the courageous work of Rachel Carson and the environmental movement in the 1960s, regulation was forced on them. In the 1980s, as their next line of products was being developed, these chemical companies took preemptive action to avoid the effective regulation of agricultural biotechnology.

In late 1986, George H. W. Bush was vice president and the Reagan administration was fully engaged in deregulation throughout the federal government. There were no GMO crops on the market, but the Monsanto Corporation had big plans for biotechnology. At the White House, Bush played host to four executives of Monsanto, who wanted to make sure that the regulatory system worked in their favor. They got what they wanted. In 1992, when Bush was president, his vice president, Dan Quayle, announced the government's plans for regulatory "reform" at a press conference in the Indian Treaty Room near his office. It was called "the coordinated framework," and it was a real coup for industry. It left just enough oversight in place to give the public the appearance that the government was involved but gave regulators no meaningful role.

This is how it works. Three federal agencies are involved: the

Food and Drug Administration (FDA), with responsibility for food and drugs; the Environmental Protection Agency (EPA), charged with overseeing all pesticides; and the Animal and Plant Health Inspection Service (APHIS), an agency of the USDA, which controls field testing. These agencies work independently and do not coordinate their activities. The framework announced by Quayle said that no new laws would be passed to regulate biotechnology, and since then no new legislation has been passed by Congress. Meanwhile, the federal agencies charged with oversight use laws passed decades ago that were created for entirely different purposes and based on the best science available at the time.

The USDA relies on the Plant Pest Act, which excludes the process of genetic engineering from consideration and narrowly defines plant pests. It issues permits through a simple notification process. In theory, the USDA could ask companies to evaluate the ecological risks of their field tests, but in practice it relies on these companies to volunteer information that would lead to further assessment. Not surprisingly, a review of over 8,000 field test results showed that not one resulted in an environmental assessment. After the field test is done, the crop is deregulated and the USDA has no more authority over it. No monitoring or further field testing is required, regardless of the environmental risks the crop may pose. All three agencies operate passively under a "don't tell, don't look" policy. If the industry doesn't tell the government about a potential risk, the government doesn't look for it.

The EPA makes an effort to control the environmental impacts of the GMOs it regulates, but it's limited to only one kind of GMO, those that contain pesticides. And it can act only within the confines of the Federal Insecticide, Fungicide, and Rodenticide Act and the Toxic Substances Control Act, both of which were designed to deal with toxins, not living organisms that replicate themselves. The EPA also disregards the process used to create GMOs. It assumes that the use of Bt—*Bacillus thuringiensis,* a pesticide commonly used in GMO plants—is safe. It is safe, but only when the bacillus is used in its natural form, as a foliar spray. Genetically engineered *Bt* is not the same; it's engineered into a shorter form and permanently switched on. While natural *Bt* is activated only in the guts of susceptible insects, GMO *Bt* is always active and constantly exuded from all parts of the plant. Transgenic *Bt* is known to adversely affect soil microorganisms and harm beneficial insect populations. But because the EPA doesn't take the engineering process into consideration, the genetic changes that are made to the *Bt* are ignored.

The FDA regulates GMOs under the Food, Drug, and Cosmetic Act. If something can be "generally regarded as safe" (GRAS) under the act, as most conventional foods are, then it is not regulated. Dr. Michael Hansen of Consumers Union says that the extraordinary decision by the FDA to consider all genetically engineered food, prior to being studied, to be GRAS weakens consumer safety requirements, because manufacturers no longer have to establish the safety of these products before selling them. The American public, Hansen points out, falsely assumes that the FDA does premarket safety testing. In actuality, the companies only engage in a voluntary and informal "consultation process" with the FDA. As a result, the GMOs that are on grocery store shelves today have never been tested for human health hazards.

Henry Miller, who was head of biotechnology at the FDA from 1979 to 1994, told the *New York Times* in 2001 that government agencies did "exactly what big agribusiness had asked them to do and told them to do." During Miller's tenure at the FDA, staff scientists warned about food safety concerns and called for further testing. According to Steven Druker, a public-interest lawyer who obtained internal FDA memos produced at the time, "References to the unintended negative effects of bioengineering were progressively deleted from drafts of the policy statement." Druker said he found out, for instance, that tests were done on the first GMO food ever commercialized, the Flavr Savr tomato. It failed to pass these trials, but instead of resolving the toxicological questions that the tests raised, the FDA disregarded the results. Other FDA documents that warned of hazards, such as

concerns about the use of antibiotic resistance markers, were ignored. The man in charge of policy at the FDA at the time was
Michael Taylor, who had been a lawyer for Monsanto.

Taylor has rotated back and forth between industry and government more than once. This is the "revolving door" through
which industry employees pass in and out of government. The
close relationship between these regulators and their regulated
industries has compromised the independence of government.
Beth Burrows, a longtime champion of using independent science
to evaluate biotechnology and promote biosafety, runs the Edmonds Institute in Edmonds, Washington. For years the institute's website offered a searchable database of industry-related
personnel who were working in the federal government. But Burrows says her staff had to stop doing the revolving-door list because "the volume of submissions under the Bush administration
became so great, and things were getting so bad, it would have
been easier to do a list of government officials who were not coming through the revolving door."

There is another reason that the regulating agencies do not respond to evidence of harm. Early on, they made a preemptive decision to approve all GMOs on the basis of a concept known as
"substantial equivalence." The biotechnology industry created a
blanket exemption for its products by simply declaring, without any scientific basis, that those products were the same as
their natural counterparts. In an article published in the science
journal *Nature*, Erik Millstone calls substantial equivalence "a
pseudo-scientific concept...a commercial and political judgment
masquerading as if it were scientific...[that] was created primarily to provide an excuse for not requiring biochemical or toxicological tests." Millstone maintains that legislators never agreed
on a meaning for the term and yet it continues to act "as a barrier to further research into the possible risks of eating GMOs."
Agricultural economist Charles Benbrook says that the most important thing to understand about the idea of substantial equivalence is that it "was formed well before many of today's most
important risk concerns had been studied to any significant de-

gree." However, we now know that GMOs are causing environmental damage and may be harming human health.

The regulatory system we have today is the same one, with some minor exceptions, that was adopted in the early 1990s. It effectively exempted this one industry from our most important environmental and consumer protection laws, which guarantee our right to know what is in the products we consume and our right to sue manufacturers when the government fails to protect our safety. Even though public-opinion polls repeatedly show that well over 90 percent of Americans want labels on genetically engineered foods, those labels are not allowed. Many European and Asian countries label GMOs, and the manufacturers have no problem in complying with those laws. Labels provide consumers a choice and can be used to trace products that prove to be hazardous. Americans with food sensitivities or religious or other dietary restrictions can't avoid unwanted genetically altered organisms. What's a vegan to do with a bowl of fresh strawberries that have fish genes in them?

The real hypocrisy of the industry's position on safety is revealed in the contrast between what its representatives say and what the government says. The FDA's Statement of Policy, published in the *Federal Register* in 1992, says, "Ultimately, it is the food producer who is responsible for assuring safety." The industry position is captured in a statement made by Monsanto's director of corporate communications, who said, "Monsanto should not have to vouchsafe the safety of biotech food. Our interest is in selling as much of it as possible. Assuring its safety is the FDA's job."

Better Safe Than Sorry?

While we know enough to be concerned, we still don't know as much as we should about the risks GMOs pose. Blame for that can be placed squarely on our flawed regulatory system. A peer-reviewed paper published in 2004 examined nearly one hundred sources, including regulatory documents and unpublished studies by industry, and concluded that approval in the United States is "a rubber-stamp process" designed to "increase public confidence in, but not ensure the safety of, genetically engineered foods." The study found that industry used surrogate proteins for its studies instead of the GMOs people actually consumed, that no long-term animal feeding tests were done, and that test conditions were manipulated to get the desired results. One of the study's authors, Dr. David Schubert, a cell biologist at the Salk Institute in California, said that U.S. regulators relied almost exclusively on information supplied by companies that had not been published or subjected to peer review.

In 2005, the USDA's own inspector general issued a report chastising them for a long list of inadequacies, such as not knowing what was done with GMO crops and failing to monitor field trials, including trials of highly experimental transgenic plants engineered to produce chemicals and drugs. Two large harvests of pharmaceutical crops were left in storage without the USDA's knowledge or approval. Because the department did not monitor field tests adequately, it could not enforce regulations or hold applicants responsible for unauthorized releases of GMOs. The report said that the USDA had permitted 49,300 field tests since 1986 but still lacked basic information about these tests, such as where they took place.

British geneticist Mae-Wan Ho says the flaws in the regulatory system, both in the United States and in the United Kingdom, present a scientific "nightmare," because there are now at least a dozen studies showing that GMOs are hazardous to human and environmental health. The problem, she says, is that our current regulatory systems rely on risk assessment, a policy that allows regulators to collude with industry and ignore the evidence.

Risk assessment is a decision-making technique that was created in the 1960s, when we realized that we needed to develop some quantifiable standards to regulate the discharge of industrial poisons into the environment. The first step in risk assessment is identifying and describing a hazard that a product might present. Then the hazard's level of severity, exposure rate, likelihood of occurrence, and scale are quantified. These calculations define the risk, which is then compared to costs and benefits. The official formula for conducting a risk assessment was published in 1983 by the National Academy of Sciences.

Ideally, risk assessment is science-based and the results are stated as a range of possibilities about what might happen. The reality is that risk assessment involves uncertainty, and scientists often disagree about testing methods and results. There are arguments about basic assumptions, design parameters, sample size, bias, elements of chance, errors, the time and place of the study, the credentials of the principal investigators, and the source of the study's funding and institutional support. All of this has become so fraught that bureaucrats can argue for years about technicalities even when it becomes clear that a chemical—dioxin, for instance—is highly toxic and harmful. In the meantime, nothing is done. Anyone who is aware of the toxic soup that our environment has become, or who is concerned about the increasing burden of chemicals we all carry around in our bodies, knows how inadequate the policy of risk assessment has become.

Dr. Sheldon Krimsky of Tufts University writes that "the release of GMOs into the environment offers a unique challenge to risk assessment because the effects of microorganisms are not as obvious as those of plants or animals; [they] reproduce quickly and are impossible to recall; [and] unlike nutrients, toxins and pollutants, microorganisms can reproduce and move about the environment on their own; and microorganisms exchange their DNA with other species quite readily adding to the complexity of risk assessment." Krimsky points out that our system of regulation "has moved toward a cost-benefit approach that places low priority on the protection of natural habitats per se and is moving rapidly toward a clear and present danger standard to justify regulatory intervention."

The most widely accepted alternative to risk assessment is the precautionary principle. It holds that governments have an affirmative duty to take preventive measures to avoid harm. It's often called the "better safe than sorry" principle, because it allows lawmakers to take action even if the science is uncertain. The precautionary principle is now embedded in an array of international environmental treaties, including the International Biosafety Protocol, adopted in Montreal, Canada, in 2002.

Risk assessment requires some "proof" of harm, usually expressed in predictive numbers like how many people will die of cancer if a chemical is released, before regulatory measures are taken. It can allow unsubstantiated allegations of scientific uncertainty to postpone the imposition of controls on activities that may already be harming the environment or the public health. The precautionary principle is like risk assessment in that it first requires that a hazard be identified and evaluated using the best scientific tools available, but it operates differently in several important respects. It allows action to be taken to prevent harm, and it takes into consideration long-term and cumulative effects. Most important, it shifts the burden of proof to the proponents of an activity or developers of a product, to show that it will not cause harm or at least to monitor and evaluate its performance over time.

Lawyer Carolyn Raffensperger compares the precautionary principle to the Golden Rule of Christianity and rabbinical law, which, she says, comes down to treating others as you would be treated and refraining from doing what you would not want done. "Humility," Raffensperger says, "would stand us in good stead here, because we do not know all the consequences of engineering species." Raffensperger regrets that "ethical questions are seldom welcome in policy circles. We are told to leave our values at the door and make decisions on the basis of science."

The lack of a meaningful regulatory system means that private interests are in the position of making decisions about how potentially dangerous technologies are used. Corporations are about making money, not moral decisions. And yet they use their wealth to wield political influence, and as such are taking responsibility for our health and safety whether they want to admit it or not. As one long-time critic of the industry, author and lawyer Andrew Kimbrell, points out, "The technologies we choose to implement determine much of who we are and what we do as a society." In the case of GMOs, because of the way that their manufacturers have behaved in imposing them on us, Kimbrell says, this technology *is* legislation.

Responsibility for the lack of meaningful regulation lies with the agrochemical companies, with the regulators, and with those scientists who from the beginning wanted to avoid public scrutiny. Science historian Susan Wright says that it was understood early on that if scientists were not "seen to act, legislators would likely move to investigate and regulate this emerging field." Their decision to regulate themselves facilitated the industry's success with politicians, who were then easily persuaded to go along with self-regulation. Wright says this was done with "shaky scientific reasoning. As commercial investments took off in the late 1970s, the voluntary controls proposed by U.S. scientists and promulgated by the National Institutes of Health all but disappeared." Not all scientists supported this outcome, and now, with mounting evidence raising new safety concerns, even the pro-biotechnology members of the National Academy of Science are saying that the regulatory system should be strengthened.

My concern with the way the regulatory system was undermined is that it has allowed the biotechnology industry to impose "full-spectrum dominance" over seeds in all realms, from the biological to the political. Many people either believe that GMO foods are tested and safe or simply don't know that 80 percent of the processed foods sitting on their grocery store shelves contain GMOs. In the meantime, multinational agribusiness companies have insinuated their patented and genetically engineered organisms into our food supply. But the apparent success of this strategy does not mean that GMOs are inevitable. Part of the mythology behind the industrialization and globalization of agriculture is the notion that these commercial technologies are the foundation of our economic progress. In reality, these technologies are undermining the natural wealth of agriculture by extinguishing agricultural diversity and harming the environment.

Industrial agriculture is not economically or ecologically vibrant, and it suffers from what Fowler and Mooney call "the plague of sameness." Fortunately, this grip on the uniformity of mind and seed is loosening, and resistance to it is growing.

The Seed Insurgency

The impulse to save seeds runs deep in the human psyche. And as often happens during political repression, responses entail acts of enormous courage. British journalist Fred Pearce covered the story of the destruction of the seed bank at Abu Ghraib. He calls Iraq's ancient seed "the genetic holy grail, the ark of the lost seeds, the future of agricultural prosperity of Iraq." He discovered that just before the U.S. invasion, a few Iraqi scientists hurriedly packed up what seeds they could save and shipped them to a seed bank in Syria. Pearce went to Syria to find out what had happened to the container of seeds, called the "black box." When he finally located it at the International Center for Agricultural Research in Dry Areas (ICARDA) in Aleppo, he says, he was disappointed to find that it was "just a battered old brown cardboard box sealed with tape, sitting on a shelf in a refrigerator."

ICARDA, which is working to help reestablish agriculture in both Afghanistan and Iraq, says it will use Iraq's seed to provide Iraqi farmers with crops already adapted to their area, plants that over time have developed a natural resistance to extreme heat and local pests. Decades of conflict in both places make farming difficult and regional plant breeding almost impossible. Nothing we save can possibly replace what farmers could do if they were allowed to grow their own seed. But, Pearce says, these small efforts are "like zoos—they're not a substitute for having wild animals but they can help preserve them till we sort out what we can do."

Courageous acts of seed saving occurred during World War II as well. In 1940, the most important seed collection in the world was housed in what is now called the Vavilov Institute in Leningrad, Russia. It held over 200,000 accessions and was named for the great plant explorer Nikolai Ivanovich Vavilov. By 1941, the siege of Leningrad was under way; it eventually caused 600,000 deaths due to starvation. At first staff scientists at the institute prepared duplicates of half the collection to be sent out of the country. They packed the seeds and their valuable library onto a train, but it never broke through the siege line. As time wore on, researchers guarded what they could, patrolled the deserted institute, put out fires, and killed rats. Finally the institute was evacuated, and each staff member was given a small packet of seeds to keep. From July 1941 to October 1942, ninety-eight research scientists left the institute, and ten of them died in the siege.

It is said that fourteen stayed behind, living inside the institute to guard what was left. They struggled to survive in the unheated rooms. One survivor later wrote that they could see by light reflected by tin boxes covered with hoarfrost. But moisture and rodents destroyed more and more seed samples. Several staff members died of starvation, surrounded by bags of rice, potatoes, and other food. They'd refused to eat the seed, believing that one day it would be needed to replenish their war-torn land.

In his poem "The Seed Keepers," Palestinian journalist Fawaz Turki captured the spirit of a people who have been living in a time of conflict and losing their olive orchards, farms, and homelands. He wrote, "I do not fear your tyranny. I guard one seed of a tree my forefathers have saved that I shall plant again, in my homeland."

TWO

Trespass

My generation, or perhaps the one preceding mine,
has been the first to engage, under the leadership of
the exact sciences, in a destructive colonial warfare
against nature. The future will curse us for it.

ERWIN CHARGAFF, *the father
of molecular biology*

Waimea, Kauaʻi, Hawaiʻi

The first European to enter the Kingdom of Hawaiʻi was Captain
James Cook. He landed on the west side of the island of Kauaʻi in
January 1778. Cook was already several years into his third ex-
ploratory voyage around the Pacific as commander of two British
ships, the *Resolution* and the *Discovery*. Of all the Pacific island
nations he had visited, Hawaiʻi, he found, was a place of incom-
parable beauty and abundance. His journals were not usually ef-
fusive, but on his first visit to Hawaiʻi he wrote that the flowers
"sent forth the most fragrant smell I had any where met with,"
the taro was "the best I ever tasted," the sweet potatoes were the
largest, the canoes were "shaped and fitted with more judgment
than any I had before seen," and the people were "open, can-
did, active . . . and traded on the most favorable terms of any in the
Pacific."

That was probably the last time Hawaiians and Westerners
dealt with each other on anything like equal terms. Following

Cook, the islands were invaded by whalers, sugar barons, and missionaries bringing with them disease, economic exploitation, and colonialism. Two hundred years after Cook's arrival, on the island of Oʻahu, another invasion began.

In 1972, while attending a conference in Honolulu, Herbert Boyer, a University of California biochemist, and Stanley Cohen, a Stanford University geneticist, were chatting over sandwiches. They suddenly realized that they could combine their work and do something that had never been done before: recombine DNA from different species and create a new organism. Until that singular moment, the general rule of evolution was that species maintained strong biological boundaries. Now technology was about to extend the hand of man into the molecular world and assume the power to create new life on earth.

Hawaiʻi is both the birthplace of biotechnology and its nursery. Agrochemical corporations like Monsanto, Dow, Syngenta/Garst, and DuPont/Pioneer Hi-Bred test and grow genetically engineered crops on all five major islands. Some of these crops have been highly experimental, such as sugar cane engineered with human genes. At one time Monsanto had 85 of the 143 active permits for experimental crops, spread out over several islands. Overall, almost 2,000 permits for open-air field testing of GMOs have been issued for Hawaiʻi, far more than for any other state. Thousands of acres of GMOs have been grown in Hawaiʻi by seven biotechnology companies and three universities. Hawaiʻi offers them a benevolent year-round growing season that can produce three crops a year. And it has a favorable business climate. By 2006, the State of Hawaiʻi had committed more than $185 million in technology tax credits to biotech companies.

The *Honolulu Advertiser* reports that biotechnology industry jobs actually cost the state an estimated $30 million in lost tax revenues. Each company can write off up to $2 million in taxes without actually having to create jobs. Technology jobs in Hawaiʻi fell 2.7 percent between 2001 and 2004, and wages paid are below national averages, even though the local cost of living is high. Still, the GMO industry in Hawaiʻi enjoys a reputation as contributing to the economy. It is allowed to use public lands intended to benefit Native Hawaiians and former sugar plantation land for its crops. The transgenic seed industry has become the state's new plantation agriculture.

Syngenta and Pioneer have their headquarters on the west side of Kaua'i, not far from where Cook first landed. Kaua'i is known as "the Garden Island" because most of it is lush and wet, but this part of the island is dry. Its deep, rich red soil and fresh water make it an ideal place to grow corn. Except for the sugar cane, it looks like the Midwest, with mile after mile of corn, soybeans, and even sunflowers growing along the roads. Long lines of rental cars snake past the monument to Cook in Waimea, on their way to Waimea Canyon, a 4,000-foot chasm that Mark Twain dubbed the "Grand Canyon of the Pacific." Some island residents say that the tourists should be warned about what's being grown on Kaua'i, and even suggest that the welcome sign at the airport be changed to read WELCOME TO THE MUTANT GARDEN ISLAND.

Visitors who come to the island for vacation don't see the experimental GMO crops being grown here. But the locals often stumble on the tiny plots, some no bigger than an average bathroom, tucked inside coffee plantations or hidden behind rusting sugar mills. GMO seed crops are grown openly in larger fields, often next to vacation condominiums at Po'ipu Beach or across from an upscale shopping mall in Lihue. You can buy a book on the dangers of eating genetically engineered food at the Borders bookstore there and go outside to watch it being grown.

Low-Hanging Fruit

The University of Hawai'i developed, patented, and then, in 1998, released transgenic papaya trees that were resistant to the ringspot virus. Soon after their introduction in Puna, on the Big Island, these trees began contaminating other papaya varieties. (GMO contamination can occur through cross-pollination as well as when GMOs are mixed with conventional plants and seeds. Contamination can take place when wind, insects, plants, animals, and other vectors move GMO pollen from plant to plant. Or it can happen when seeds are spread by humans, wind, or insects and grow into transgenic plants that then breed with conventional plants.) Organic papaya growers and backyard gardeners began to worry that they would lose their wild and hearty trees as transgenic papaya trees spread. Tourists became unwitting partners in the GMO contamination whenever they tossed out seeds from the unlabeled GMO papayas they bought in grocery stores. By 2004, almost 50 percent of papayas tested on the Big Island were contaminated.

When the transgenic papaya was first introduced, the biotechnology industry took out full-page color ads in national newspapers bragging about how it had saved the ailing Hawaiian papaya industry. In fact, the GMO papaya performed poorly in the marketplace. Exports have plummeted, and farmers have lost trees and business. A group called GMO Free Hawaii says that the economic situation on the islands is becoming especially perilous for organic farmers because of GMO contamination. Now they also face the prospect of GMO bananas, sugar cane, and pineapples. Fortunately, the coffee industry in Hawai'i has rejected GMO coffee, joining other agricultural groups, like California's premium rice and wine associations, that have said no to GMO crops.

The biotech industry is desperate for a success story. In the fifteen years that GMO foods have been on the market, the industry has not released one product that benefits consumers. Aside from the papaya, only two GMO crops have penetrated the market: herbicide-resistant plants and pesticidal plants. These are used exclusively by commodity farmers, who for the most part are dependent on government subsidies to make ends meet. GMOs can penalize other farmers. When organic and conventional crops are contaminated with GMOs, they have to be pulled up, burned, or sold as transgenic crops, which bring the lowest prices. Organic and conventional farmers now have to pay more for their seed to be certified GMO-free. They have to install elaborate systems of separation to keep GMOs out of their crops and bear the costs of testing—which can amount to $300 per test. And they lose export markets that shun GMOs. The American Farm Bureau estimates that U.S. farmers lose $300 million a year because the European Union (EU) will not accept U.S. corn.

Between 1999 and 2001, GMO crops cost the U.S. economy $12 billion, says the UK's Soil Association. Its report also says that U.S. farm subsidies, which were meant to be reduced, have actually risen because of the overproduction of GMO crops, costing U.S. taxpayers an extra $3 to $5 billion annually. When GMOs that have not been approved for human consumption contaminate the food supply, the public shares the costs of investigating and cleaning up the mess. All of this does not include the costs farmers have incurred because of crop failures in genetically engineered cotton and soybeans.

By any measure, agriculture is not better off now than it was fifteen years ago, when the growing of transgenic crops began. Overall, biotechnology (including its medical and agricultural uses) has lost something like $100 billion since it was first invented, says Arthur Levinson, the chief executive of one of the industry's most successful pioneer companies, Genentech. Levinson was quoted in the *New York Times* as telling industry analysts that biotechnology has been "one of the biggest money-losing industries in the history of mankind."

Lessons from Starlink

Starlink corn is a good example of how a single transgenic organism can quickly contaminate the entire food supply. In 2000 it was discovered in taco shells, setting off a massive food recall that eventually reached three hundred corn products, including white corn, sweet corn, and popcorn. Starlink was used for animal feed but was not approved for human consumption because it could cause an allergic reaction. Aventis, the manufacturer of Starlink, spent $150 million on cleanup in the United States, but its GMO was soon found in corn shipments to Japan and South Korea, which cost U.S. farmers those markets for a while. Then, in 2002, Starlink was found in products donated as food aid to Bolivia, and the UN World Food Programme found it in food-aid corn in Central America in 2005. Either decontamination is not possible or it was not done well, or the leftover Starlink was simply dumped on the poor.

Starlink has taught us a lot about contamination. For one thing, it was planted on less than one half of 1 percent of all the acreage planted to corn in the United States, but it got into the entire corn supply. The reason is that our industrial food system constantly mixes grains during processing and shipping, making it impossible to keep unwanted organisms under control. Another interesting aspect of this story is that this contamination was not detected by the industry or the government. They have no mechanisms in place, and no motivation, to check for GMO contamination. It was found by consumer activists, who later revealed that Aventis and the seed companies that sold Starlink did not make sure that farmers took special precautions with this product that would keep it separate.

Consumer groups contend that Aventis knew this contamination could easily happen but failed to prevent it. Aventis adamantly denies this and blames the farmers. Eventually what Aventis did to correct the problem was to ask the USDA to approve Starlink as fit for human consumption retroactively, effectively defining the problem out of existence. This had the added benefit of ensuring that the company would avoid further liability. Depending on one's point of view, Aventis—now Bayer CropScience—did or did not learn something from the Starlink fiasco.

Bayer CropScience's déjà vu experience came on August 18, 2006, when the USDA announced that its Liberty Link 601 herbicide-resistant rice, which was not approved for commercial use, had been detected in U.S. long-grain rice. Again the contamination was not found by industry or the government. This time it was found by an export customer. And even though word soon reached the USDA, it took the department three weeks to announce it to the public. The time lapse was blamed on the difficulty investigators had in getting the genetic information they needed to identify the experimental rice from Bayer CropScience. This contamination incident eventually affected the entire U.S. long-grain rice industry and spread to six states.

What did Bayer do? It asked the USDA to approve the rice retroactively. And the USDA, after accepting Bayer's safety data on LL601 long-grain rice, a third of which was redacted from public versions of the documents, retroactively approved it. Then, as soon as Bayer got back-door approval for its GMO rice, it began commercializing it in the Philippines.

By obtaining post-contamination approval of some of their most troublesome products and by allowing contamination from their products to spread, these companies are undermining the integrity of the world's seed supply. The industry wants the world to accept what it euphemistically calls the "adventitious presence" of transgenes. Instead of holding the line at zero tolerance for transgenic material, which is what the organic farming community and many consumers and environmentalists want, government regulators are adopting the biotechnology-industry-friendly definition of "GMO-free" as the presence of .09 percent or less of transgenic material.

Meanwhile, the U.S. rice industry is still staggering from the blow dealt by Bayer's LL601. California rice farmer Greg Massa says, "August eighteenth is our September eleventh." The price of rice futures plummeted, at a cost of $150 million. Japan slammed the door on long-grain rice, and the EU market may close permanently. Now conventional rice farmers have to pay for continuous testing, and there have been more recalls, more losses, and a growing number of lawsuits from farmers in the southern states who were affected by the contamination. The $200 million California rice industry clings to its image as a producer of high-quality rice in order to get a premium price. During the LL601 scare it tested every crop to ensure that its rice was clean and to reassure its customers in Asia. Then, in 2007, the California rice industry decided that GMO rice should not be grown in the state at all, because these two forms of agriculture, genetically altered and conventional, cannot coexist.

Roundup Ready Nation

The most widely grown GMO crop is Monsanto's Roundup Ready soybean, a soybean engineered to withstand being sprayed with Monsanto's best-selling herbicide, Roundup. When farmers spray their herbicide-resistant crops, the weeds die but the crop survives. Getting plants to do this trick means fewer weeds for farmers and more sales of Roundup for Monsanto. As of August 2006, 89 percent of the soybeans, 65 percent of the cotton, and 36 percent of the corn planted in the United States were herbicide-resistant (HR). In the first nine years HR crops were planted, herbicide use increased dramatically. A study done by the former head of the Board of Agriculture for the National Academy of Sciences found that farmers who planted Roundup Ready soybeans used two to five times more herbicides than farmers who planted conventional soybeans.

The harmful effects of herbicides are well documented, and evidence of the toxicity of Roundup is beginning to emerge. It used to be considered relatively safe, but now the Danish government has banned its use, and it has been linked to deaths in Japan and farm-worker illnesses in California. Herbicides pollute water and soil and cause health problems for humans and animals. According to a study cited in the journal *Science*, herbicides used on GMOs are "clear-cutting" farm fields, eliminating weeds and other seed-bearing plants that birds feed on and threatening bird populations. The study found that one European songbird population had fallen by 90 percent since the introduction of GMO crops. For Hawai'i, the world's epicenter of species extinction and the world's leading hot spot of critical concern over biodiversity, the constant spraying of herbicides on sugar and pineapple plantations, golf courses, and now on all the GMO test sites is a critical problem.

Herbicides are used so much now that weeds are developing resistance to them. Some weeds have picked up resistance by crossing with HR crops. In Canada, for instance, weeds that are resistant to three different herbicides have been found. For that to happen, they had to hybridize with three different GMOs. They can then go on to cross with other nearby weeds and spread their herbicide resistance, giving pollution a life of its own. These "superweeds" have now been found in six states and several other countries.

So far, nine species of weeds are known to have developed resistance to Roundup. A study done by Syngenta says that HR weeds are the number-one concern of farm managers and that in some places they've decreased farmland property values by 17 percent. Farmers are also becoming concerned that they will have to use stronger and even more expensive chemicals for weed control. Monsanto says not to worry—it will come up with new herbicides that will take care of the problem. Meanwhile, the chemical industry has recommended using paraquat and 2,4-D, both highly toxic chemicals that are banned in many countries.

The second most popular transgenic crops are insecticidal plants engineered with *Bt,* mainly corn and cotton. Instead of resulting in an overall reduction in the use of pesticides, these crops are not effective substitutes for chemical insect controls. Observations in this country and a Cornell University study of cotton farmers in China have shown that just as much insecticide is being used on *Bt* cotton crops now as was used on cotton crops before GMOs were introduced.

Worse, the National Research Council says that "the evolution of resistance to *Bt* crops is inevitable." Thus, the insect world is beginning to form resistance to GMOs as well. These insecticidal crops are constantly leaking recombinant *Bt* from their stalks, leaves, and roots into their surroundings. It stays active in the soil for months, and *Bt* in pollen is known to kill both targeted pests and beneficial insects like lacewings. It has been implicated in killing monarch butterflies and has been suggested as one possible cause of the massive and unexplained die-off of bee colonies.

The problem is, GMO manufacturers are a chemical industry posing as agriculture. They say they are about creating life. Their ads always show happy faces and healthy plants. But what they're really about is death, the poisoning of weeds and insects. Transgenic plants are created by agrochemical companies and used in the same way that those companies' chemicals are used: as pest controls. If these plants were treated as chemicals, they might be handled more carefully.

Sex, Lies, and Invasiveness

Between 1999 and 2005, there were 115 documented cases of GMO contamination, twice as many in the United States as in any other country. GMO contamination happens when unapproved GMOs are found or when approved GMOs are found where they don't belong. The GMOs in our food aren't considered contamination. The problem is, GMOs are biological brats. They simply will not stay put. They don't behave. They cross with other plants through sexual reproduction, their pollen gets spread around by the wind, birds, insects, and rodents, and they mix with other crops. As a result, the Union of Concerned Scientists (UCS) reported in 2004 that the conventional seed supply was now "pervasively contaminated" with transgenic DNA. One laboratory UCS used for its tests found that up to 83 percent of conventional corn, soy, and canola seed they tested was contaminated. As a result, even farmers who think they are planting conventional crops are actually spreading GMOs.

The USDA sets separation distances for field tests that are supposed to prevent GMO contamination, although it's common knowledge that they don't work as intended. One study, using just 269 plants on one tenth of an acre for ninety days, showed that pollen traveled well beyond the 900 feet set by the USDA as a separation requirement. The USDA even expressed surprise when genes from Roundup Ready creeping bentgrass at an experimental test site in Oregon had pollinated plants 13 miles away. Because bentgrass can cross-pollinate with at least twelve other species of grass, the Forest Service (an agency of the USDA) was alarmed by these findings. It says that GMO bentgrass contamination could adversely affect all 175 national forests and grasslands.

Time after time, the regulators can't even do the little that is asked of them. In 2002, for instance, Pioneer Hi-Bred in Kaua'i was fined for violating its EPA permit requirements. It was told to check its plots and report back, because the EPA wanted to make sure that Pioneer's transgenic corn did not contaminate nearby fields. The following year Pioneer again failed to report, and again it was fined. Eventually the company submitted its data, which said that no new contamination had been found. The EPA, relying on what it was told, said it was satisfied. Except it just so happens that there *was* transgenic contamination in Pioneer's corn fields that year. The contamination came from plots of GMOs regulated by the USDA. Remember, the EPA is concerned only with pesticidal plants. So if the contamination is not from a pesticidal plant test plot, the EPA can disregard it. The EPA said it wasn't concerned about contamination from the USDA fields. The company, for its part, said it was in regulatory compliance. In the meantime, GMOs in their fields were contaminating one another.

In Hawai'i, the business community considers biotechnology to be a part of the state's agricultural economy and not a polluting industry. A few years ago the Hawai'i Crop Improvement Association (HCIA), the state's biotechnology industry association, went around to schools promoting biotechnology in the classroom. It handed out packets of *Bt* sweet corn to children, to take home and plant. Planting *Bt* corn in this way would violate the environmental laws governing the way insecticidal corn should be used. Nothing was done to reprimand them by state or federal agencies. This careless attitude toward GMO contamination is often exhibited by both industry and government regulators.

In a recent court case involving Roundup Ready alfalfa, a federal judge said that the USDA had grown "cavalier" about laws meant to protect the environment from the adverse effects of these crops and noted the increasing problem of herbicide-resistant weeds. In its February 2007 ruling, the court found that the USDA had failed to assess the environmental impacts of Monsanto's alfalfa before deregulating it in 2005. Alfalfa is the fourth-largest crop grown in the United States and provides a huge market for Monsanto's seeds and chemicals, so this was a big setback for the company. It was a remarkable win for the farmers who brought the case. They have been dealing with GMO contamination of their crops and the loss of export markets like Japan, where GMOs are not approved, as well as the loss of the domestic non-GMO market. The judge understood that non-GMO crops are an important part of the country's agricultural economy and that organic and conventional farmers' sales are being hurt by GMO contamination.

In itself, gene flow is not necessarily harmful. What matters is the kind of molecule that's moving around, where it goes, and how it behaves once it gets there. When transgenes used to modify one plant move into another plant, they can become unstable and behave unpredictably. When natural genes do this, they are governed by biological rules that organisms have developed over millennia to deal with gene flow and to keep species separate. When artificially engineered genes do this, however, different rules come into play. Genetic engineering by definition overcomes these rules in order to create new genes and organisms. Genetic engineering is the very essence of invasiveness, by design.

For twenty years, Professor Norman Ellstrand, director of the Biotechnology Impacts Center at the University of California at Riverside, has been asking the question, "When genes wander, should we worry?" He says we used to think that our food crops, which have been so highly developed, could no longer cross with their wild relatives. He studied rice, canola, and sunflowers to see if they were likely to cross with their wild relatives and if they might acquire a fitness advantage by doing so. His concern was that when herbicide-resistant crops cross with related weeds, the weeds might become heartier as well as herbicide-resistant. Ellstrand found that there was a high level of hybridization between wild and food crops—up to 40 percent— and he found that those hybrids set 15 percent more seed than the wild plants did.

All crops were once wild plants. To retain their genetic fitness they need the diversity of genes in their wild relatives. The contamination of weeds and wild relatives of crops with GMOs will have a devastating impact on the genetic diversity of agriculture, because it will reduce both the genetic variability and the integrity of these plants. Ellstrand says that he is concerned about this and that the only way to contain the problem is to take strong preventive measures. But as another academic report concluded, "The movement of transgenes beyond their intended destination is a virtual certainty." Unlike chemical pollution, which can be diluted or cleaned up, genetic pollution is irreversible. Once GMOs get out, they can't be recalled. And some transgenic plants are far more promiscuous than their natural counterparts. Research at the University of Chicago, published in *Nature*, found that one transgenic plant was twenty times more likely to interbreed with its wild relatives than its nontransgenic cousin.

Monsanto, Syngenta, Pioneer/DuPont, and Bayer now have over a decade of experience with contamination. They have been fined, chastised by consumers, and sued by farmers, but they have done nothing about the contamination problem. The industry's position is that if people want to avoid GMOs, they have to figure out how to avoid them. As one industry critic noted, "That's like saying that since Monsanto's technology is spreading a sexually transmitted disease, everyone else will have to wear a condom." Every instance of GMO contamination means that another patented organism has breached all biological, legal, political, and moral boundaries and gone somewhere it isn't wanted. Perhaps these organisms are acting as little alien messengers, trying to convince everyone that resistance to GMOs is futile. As one industry consultant put it, "The hope of industry is that over time the market is so flooded that there's nothing you can do about it. You just sort of surrender." The industry's strategy may indeed be what Dan Adolphe, from the Canadian Seed Growers Association, told a Canadian newspaper in 2002: "It's a hell of a thing to say that the way we win is we don't give the consumer a choice, but that might be it."

A Growing Concern

In 1993, before any GMO crops were commercialized, the UCS issued a report called *Perils Amidst the Promise,* a detailed analysis of the ecological risks of transgenic crops. It warned that weeds could take on herbicide-resistant genes; that GMOs would cross with wild plants, have unintended impacts on beneficial insects, produce cascading and cumulative effects, and increase the use of harmful chemicals; and that transgenic plants would become weeds themselves. The UCS said that GMOs could also contaminate traditional varieties of crops and related wild plants growing at the "centers of origin" of crops, where the plants first grew. Every one of these predictions has come about, and worse.

Eleven years later, in 2004, UCS scientists issued another report, called *A Growing Concern.* This time they were warning us about the next stage in the development of GMOs: biopharming, the use of food plants used to produce pharmaceutical and industrial chemicals. If it works, the agrochemical companies, which are allied with the pharmaceutical industry, will save millions by producing drugs in living plants instead of in factories. Plants can be made to manufacture chemicals, and industry knows how to extract them. What it does not know much about is whether these drugs will work in the human body. The human immune system tends to reject plant drugs, and they have been known to cause autoimmune disorders.

The UCS's concern this time was the environmental impacts of testing pharma crops. The report pointed out how grains are often mixed in the food supply when they are aggregated for storage or manufacture, so the use of food crops for pharmaceutical production could lead to contamination of the food supply with biopharmed chemicals. Reports of contamination by biopharmed genes have already appeared. Corn biopharmed by the ProdiGene Corporation that was genetically engineered to produce a pig vaccine contaminated soybeans intended for human consumption in Iowa, and biopharmed corn plants have appeared as volunteers in a Nebraska soybean field.

At the time of the 2004 UCS report, there were about two hundred pending applications to field-test pharma crops by fifteen companies and five universities, using crops such as rice, soybeans, corn, sugar cane, safflower, and tobacco. Experts say that food crops simply should not be used for these experiments, or if they are, they should be grown only in secure greenhouses. The processed food industry, from millers to grocers, has called for zero tolerance for biopharm contamination in food.

Meanwhile, the USDA allows biopharming in food crops to continue. Ventria Corporation was permitted to grow biopharmed rice engineered with genes from human breast milk to produce antimicrobials in open-air tests in California's rice-growing region. This experimental rice is intended for use in industrial poultry production and baby formula. It is being grown right beneath what's known as the Pacific flyway, the major path taken by millions of migratory birds and waterfowl. Nevertheless, the USDA did not require Ventria to study the impact the poultry microbicide in this crop might have on birds and wildlife, but accepted the company's assurance that it was not a problem. Although the regulatory oversight of biopharmed crops is stronger than for other GMOs, the government has not been able to keep up with the onslaught of novel products and their unknown risks. Other countries at least require that bird netting be put over open-air GMO rice trials.

In 2002, the National Academy of Science's National Research Council urged the government to give this industry more careful scrutiny. The council studied the drug avidin, which has been grown commercially and extracted from corn since 1997. Avidin has been known to kill twenty-six insect species or, at low doses, to chronically impair them. But the report noted that corn-based avidin falls through the regulatory cracks between the USDA and the EPA. That leaves farmers vulnerable, says Dan McGuire, an official with the American Corn Growers Association. McGuire says that corn farmers should be concerned about growing pharmaceutical crops because the biotech companies are not going to accept liability for any contamination that occurs, leaving farmers holding the bag.

Getting a grip on biopharming has been particularly difficult because until recently the industry has been allowed to keep the kinds of genes it uses and the locations of its experiments secret. In Hawai'i the constant tropical breezes spread pollen, seeds, and plant residue around. Families there became concerned that they might be growing food in their gardens right next to one of these experimental crops. They got together with Native Hawaiian, environmental, and consumer groups and sued for the right to know what is being grown around them. Attorney Paul Achitoff, of Earthjustice, an environmental litigation organization that represented the plaintiffs, said, "The agency entrusted with protecting human health and the environment from the impacts of genetic engineering experiments has been asleep at the wheel." In August 2006, Earthjustice and the Center for Food Safety won their lawsuit. A federal court held that the USDA had acted in "utter disregard" for the laws protecting endangered species, especially considering the extraordinary number of endangered plants and animals in Hawai'i, and ordered it to reveal the locations of its test sites. As of 2007, there has been no more biopharming in Hawai'i.

Is That a Spider in My Milk?

Food safety is always a worry. Common but deadly bacteria like *E. coli* are challenging enough, but biotechnology is taking this issue to a whole new level. Just about everything imaginable has been engineered into food plants. There is corn that produces the hepatitis B virus, corn with a human contraceptive, corn with rat genes, corn with jellyfish genes that glow in the dark, corn with chicken genes. Yum. There are growth hormones from carp genes in safflowers; human genes in tobacco, sugar cane, and rice; rat genes in soybeans; wheat genes in chickens. Goats have been engineered with spider genes so that they produce spider silk in their milk. If these strange ideas aren't enough to worry about, studies are beginning to show that the GMOs already growing all over the country in corn, soy, and canola may pose a danger to human health as well.

A study in Ireland showed that food-related diseases doubled during the same time that GMO food was introduced. The increased incidence might be caused by the acceleration of industrial agriculture, but who knows? We have lost touch with who grows our food and how it is grown, and industrial growers avoid responsibility by making it difficult to trace the origins of the ingredients in their products. If a GMO-related health problem does occur, we may not know its origins. The most frequently cited human health concern with GMOs is the possibility of serious allergic responses. GMOs are novel proteins that have never been in the human diet before, and allergies are rising everywhere. The causes are unknown. The FDA does check for potential known allergens, but even so, allergens have slipped through the system and ended up in the food supply.

Geneticist Ho has listed many health concerns related to both the products and the process used to create GMOs. She emphasizes the dangers of using antibiotic resistance markers in GMOs, which she says could create resistance to antibiotics and "leave us unable to treat major illnesses, such as the ever-problematic *E. coli.*" Echoing her worry, the British Medical Association said that "the use of antibiotic resistant marker genes in GM foodstuffs is a completely unacceptable risk, however slight, to human health."

Potential toxicity is another problem. Plants regularly produce toxins, but normally these genes are silenced. The concern is that genetic switches in GMOs could turn off this protective mechanism. Another issue is any subtle, clinically undetectable long-term effects, especially to the immune system. According to one study done in Britain, rats that were fed GMO potatoes for 100 days suffered stunted growth and damage to the immune system. Ronnie Cummins, director of the Organic Consumers Association, an organization that maintains a list of the human health risks associated with GMOs, says there is an increased risk of cancer from elevated levels of the IGF-1 factor in milk from cows treated with Monsanto's genetically engineered bovine growth hormone (rBGH). Europe and Canada have banned rBGH.

Health advocate Jeffrey Smith lists sixty-five health risks associated with everyday GMO foods in his book *Genetic Roulette*. He details dozens of alarming animal studies showing serious health problems associated with GMOs. In one, animals exclusively fed GMOs had false pregnancies, and in another, in England, 8 percent of chickens fed Aventis's T25 corn died— more than twice the national average for chicken mortality. Rats fed GMO corn had blood cell formation problems, and those fed GMO soy had liver problems, which were even worse in rats fed GMO canola. Other studies show that when *Bt* is fed to rats, it causes excessive cell growth in the digestive tract, which means it is not destroyed during digestion. When Monsanto's A-10 GMO corn was fed to rats, their immune systems went berserk, with white blood cell counts skyrocketing. When the very first GMO food, the Calgene Flavr Savr tomato, was fed to rats, they developed stomach lesions, and seven out of forty died. As Smith recounts these studies, he says there is anecdotal evidence that many animals, especially rats, when given the choice between GMO food and conventional food, refuse to eat the GMO food. He then adds that he's just trying to get us up to the level of the rats in our choices.

Before GMOs were allowed into the food supply, FDA scientists warned the agency that genetic changes could result in "undesirable alterations in the level of nutrients." Other FDA scientists advised the agency to do human and animal feeding trials. However, FDA policy is not to test or label GMOs, so the feeding trials are taking place at our dinner tables. According to a study done in Norway and Denmark, there is a serious lack of research into the human health effects of GMOs. As of 2004, only ten animal feeding studies had been published and only two of them were independent. Of the two, one showed that GMOs affected the immune system and that transgenes can transfer out of GMO food and into bacteria in the gut at detectable levels after just one meal. The other study showed evidence of precancerous conditions.

Studying these risks is a daunting and complex problem, partly because our diet is already full of GMOs. "The fact is," says microbiologist Dr. Richard Lacey, "it is virtually impossible to even conceive of a testing procedure to assess the health effects of genetically engineered foods when introduced to the food chain. Nor is there any valid nutritional or public interest reason for their introduction." The industry claims that it is "not aware of" any evidence that its products cause harm to human health. Of course, it has not looked for any evidence, either. Professor Ellstrand says there's no excuse for not assessing the risks to ourselves and the natural world. "If we have the advanced tools for creating novel agricultural products," he says, "we should use the advanced knowledge from ecology and population genetics—as well as social sciences and humanities—to make mindful choices about creating products that are best for us and our environment."

The Third Wave

As if all this weren't bad enough, there's more. Scientists are concerned about GMO pollution, which may begin to spread on an unimaginable scale and throughout every species on earth. The GMO contamination problem so far has been limited to plants, mainly annual crops. That means they are exposed to the environment for a few months and then harvested. Residue is left in the ground, and pollen gets around, and there are the GMOs that get in our guts, and all that is a concern. But wait. The worst is yet to come. The FDA is on the verge of approving transgenic fish. One distressing study showed that when just 60 transgenic fish were released into a population of 60,000 wild fish, all the wild fish were wiped out in forty generations. The authors of this study, which used computer models, said that "local extinction of a wild-type population from a release of transgenic individuals could also have cascading negative effects on the community." The concern is heightened by the fact that millions of farmed fish are accidentally released into the wild every year, so the possibility of containing transgenic fish raised on farms is slim to none.

Transgenic trees are another major ecological threat. Large plantations of transgenic trees are already being grown in the United States and elsewhere. China has planted more than a million acres of insect-resistant poplars. The forest industry wants to speed up the growth rate of trees and breed some that are easier to pulp, and it, as well as the fruit and nut industry, finds the idea of insect-resistant trees seductive.

Trees that are herbicide-resistant will be sprayed like HR plants, and that will remove the understory plants. That might be good for fire control, but HR forests have little to offer the soil or wildlife. The life of a tree involves complex interactions with its surroundings. The roots interact with the organisms in the soil; trees provide homes for animals and birds and play host to many insects. GMO forests and orchards will occupy the same space but not offer the same advantages to the environment as natural forests. And unlike annual crops, some trees can spread their pollen for up to 40 miles. One study suggested that wind can carry tree pollen for a thousand miles, something to consider when pollen and dust from China are regularly found in Southern California smog. Plus trees live for forty to four hundred years, meaning they will expose the world to their transgenes for very long periods of time.

Most GMO trees are native varieties, making them a new invasive species. Trees are more likely to cross with their wild relatives, so trees grown for pulp could destroy nearby timber forests. Trees play such a key role in regulating the environment, however, that some people have suggested that GMO trees can be used to fight global warming. But is that really an option, given the performance of transgenic crops as an environmental problem, not a solution? Because of their longevity and the critical ecological functions that trees perform, GMO trees, with all their known and unknown risks, would cause far more pollution than they could possibly address. All trees generate oxygen and digest carbon dioxide, but transgenic tree plantations would also create genetic pollution by spreading their patented genes around, decrease biodiversity, increase the use of herbicides, and contribute to the destruction of wild forests. Besides, as with most GMOs, their purpose is a hollow promise. If it's trees you want, non-transgenic trees will work just as well, without all the problems.

The example of papaya trees in Hawaiʻi demonstrates how long-lasting GMO plants can cause long-lasting problems. Stuart Pimm, author of *A Scientist Audits the Earth,* says Hawaiʻi is the place to watch to learn how all this will sort out, because it's where biodiversity comes up against the dual assaults of both human and biological colonization.

In late 2006, I visited the west side of Kauaʻi. The local newspapers at the time were full of reports about how eight children from Waimea Canyon School had been sent home sick. Twenty others had gone to the health clinic with tears in their eyes and holding their heads in their hands. As many as sixty people were affected by something—exactly what was not known. Syngenta did some spraying in a field next to the school, and teachers had been saying that they noticed strong chemical smells and had frequent health problems. There was a lot of speculation and worry about the GMOs being grown there.

What I find remarkable about this incident, which apparently is not unusual on the west side of the island, is that the growing of GMOs here has created such uneasiness. Farming used to be a welcome and healthy activity. Now, in this place where the descendants of the Hawaiians who first came into contact with the West are living, people live in fear of what's being grown around them. This small community is contending with the worst of American agriculture, not its best. They are being subjected to a level of economic and environmental exploitation that no one should have to endure. They live at ground zero for both military and agricultural testing. One day, as I was driving through the west side's GMO plantations, a low-flying aircraft from the nearby Pacific Missile Range flew by and dropped out parachutists all dressed in black, loaded with gear, who slowly drifted to the ground. Not far away, thousands of tourists were basking on the beach and playing in the surf, completely unaware that this beautiful island is the testing grounds for two of our most invasive technologies, military hardware and industrial agriculture.

In one sense, our society still seems to be operating according to eighteenth-century values of exploration and colonization. Cook, after all, took the famous botanist Joseph Banks along on his voyages to collect plants from the places he visited. The difference today is that our technologies have taken these insidious impulses to collect and devastate to unimaginable levels of destructiveness. Erwin Chargaff, who attended the birth of biotechnology, wrote an essay called "The Dangers of Genetic Engineering" in 1976. In it he expresses his regret about what the industry did with the science it developed and especially its role in genetic pollution. "You cannot recall a new form of life," he warned. "It will survive you and your children and your children's children. An irreversible attack on the biosphere is something so unheard of, so unthinkable in previous generations, that I only wish that mine had not been guilty of it."

THREE

Political Science

The corporate assault on universities has been part
of a deliberate campaign to reintroduce power onto
campuses, after the activism of the 1960's had largely
discredited corporate sponsorship.

LEONARD MINSKY, *National Coalition
for Universities in the Public Interest*

University of California, Berkeley

The morning fog had lifted, leaving a slight chill in the air. The
campus was quiet, expectant. It was late November 1998, and the
big game with Stanford was coming up. The university had called
a press conference to announce an unprecedented agreement with
Novartis, a Swiss multinational corporation, now Syngenta. Novartis was giving $25 million to Berkeley's Plant and Microbial
Biology Department. The University of California (UC) wanted
the money to fund research in plant genetics. The question hanging in the air was, did this agreement violate the university's public mission, effectively privatizing research at one of the nation's
great land-grant institutions?

The press conference was held in Koshland Hall, named for
Professor Daniel Koshland. Koshland has the unique distinction
of having been present at two of the most important scientific rev-
olutions of the twentieth century. He worked on the Manhattan
Project, which created the first nuclear weapons, and he partic-

ipated in the development of molecular biology. His namesake building is fairly typical of modern campus architecture. It's superficially attractive but has all the charm and poetry of an ice cube. Inside, the cold concrete floors and steel staircases are lit with harsh fluorescent fixtures. The entry walls display plaques with the branded names of corporate benefactors, now a common practice on college campuses. There is the Coca Cola Distinguished Professor of Marketing at the University of Arizona, the Taco Bell Distinguished Professor of Hotel and Restaurant Administration at Washington State University, and the Yahoo! Chair of Information Systems (including the exclamation point) at Stanford.

In the upstairs classroom where the press conference was held, every seat was taken. Students with bulging backpacks were sitting on the floor along the walls. Campus police stood in back, arms folded, staring straight ahead, expressionless. Novartis executives stood shoulder to shoulder with faculty members, Berkeley's chancellor, and other administration officials. They all looked on benevolently as the agreement was signed. Steven Briggs, president of Novartis Agricultural Discovery Institute, Incorporated (NADII), signed for Novartis. NADII was an "in-house" foundation, allowing Novartis to use tax-exempt funding for its research projects and, in California, to collect a 24 percent tax credit.

After Briggs signed, he looked up and announced, "This new research agreement is the final statement in academic freedom." Briggs was making a kind of ironic sense. For those opposed to the deal, the Novartis agreement was indeed "the final statement" in academic freedom—it was signaling its end. The person who had the most to say was Gordon C. Rausser, who brought Novartis to UC and was then the dean of the College of Natural Resources. This was his shining moment. He praised the Novartis deal, saying it was launching a "new research paradigm."

Suddenly there was a commotion along the wall. I was sitting in the front row, recording the press conference for radio, when I felt something rush past my head. It missed its intended target and splattered on the wall behind the front table. Another object followed, grazed Dean Rausser, and landed on the floor at his feet. It all happened in a split second, but soon it was apparent that this was a pie-throwing protest. In their hallmark style, which is humorous political theater, protesters calling themselves the Biotic Baking Brigade had tossed two vegan pumpkin pies (it was Thanksgiving week, after all) at the signers of the agreement.

Campus security guards rushed forward, wrestled the pie-throwers to the floor, and dragged them out of the room by their armpits, legs sprawled, hands cuffed, while the protesters screamed scatological objections to the Novartis deal. Dean Rausser, who was speaking at the time, raised his hand and brushed some pie off his suit. He looked around, shrugged, and smiled. I got the distinct feeling that he was actually enjoying the moment. He went on with his presentation while pie filling drooled down the wall behind him.

The protest was a brilliant move that brought national press attention to the campus controversy. Most of the opposition came from a few members of the faculty and a group called Students for Responsible Research, who denounced the agreement as an unprecedented acceleration of corporate influence on campus. Under the agreement, Novartis corporate employees were given two of the five seats on the academic committee that selected grants for funding and Novartis got first dibs on all research done by the department, not just what was funded with its money. No private corporation had penetrated a public university so far or so effectively controlled research at a single department.

The plant and microbial biology faculty liked the idea of having access to Novartis's proprietary databases, computational abilities, and money, all critical to staying competitive in molecular research. It was understood that this deal was about patents, or, as Novartis put it, the "commercialization of products." While UC dressed up the deal as a boon for California farmers, the truth is, it was a bonanza for the university and the biotechnology industry.

A report entitled "U.C. Means Business" brags about the UC system's success in private enterprise and cutting-edge technologies. Between 1995 and 2000, private funding at UC grew 77 percent. In 2003–2004, the university received $93.2 million in income from agreements with industry. In the next year, 2005, UC was awarded 424 patents, making it the national leader among universities for patent awards for the twelfth consecutive year. Patents are now a significant source of income for universities, particularly in the field of molecular biology.

The practice of allowing public universities to patent their research began in 1980, when Congress quietly passed the University and Small Business Patent Procedures Act, also known as the Bayh-Dole Act. It allowed public research institutions to work with private companies and to patent and license their inventions, even when using public money. Before, when public funding was involved, the government retained title to all innovations and shared them openly with the public, for free. Some scholars say this change was both part of the conservative agenda of the early 1980s and a backlash against the campus rebellions of the 1960s, which were, in the beginning at least, focused on issues of academic freedom.

It's now common for faculty members to work for both industry and their university at the same time. Much of the impact that private money is having on research priorities can be attributed to the fact that faculty are working both sides of the street. Many think tanks and private research centers are located near major university campuses. Every one of the nine UC campuses has a biotechnology cluster near it. The University of Texas feeds six-hundred-plus nearby high-technology companies. That might explain the annual salary of $787,319 paid to the chancellor there in 2002, 91 percent of which came from private donations.

The year before Dean Rausser brought Novartis to the Berkeley campus, he earned $1.3 million in consulting fees, billed through his private company, the Law and Economics Consulting Group. All that work had to be done on the forty-eight days a year of outside compensated activity allowed by the university.

His pay for that work amounted to $35,416 per day, while as dean he was making a comparatively minuscule $536 per day. Later that year his company conducted a $74 million public offering, worth $18 million to Rausser alone.

In the end, nothing much came out of the Novartis deal. After all the money was spent, not one patent had been optioned by Novartis. Meanwhile, public opposition to GMOs has grown, contamination incidents are costing the industry millions and hurting the farm economy, and poor returns on investments have led to a collapse of the entire "life science" strategy, which is what attracted Novartis to UC in the first place. Corporations bought, sold, and renamed themselves. Novartis merged with Zenca Agrochemicals to become Syngenta, and the successor foundation to NADII closed in 2002.

Shaky Science

There is a building on the Berkeley campus that used to be called the Life Sciences Building (LSB). It's a massive square edifice fronted by Roman columns that houses a honeycomb of offices, classrooms, and laboratories. As an undergraduate at UC, I worked as a campus tour guide, and we told visitors that LSB was constructed in two halves because it stands right over an earthquake fault. The idea was, in the event of a catastrophic earthquake, the building would slide apart rather than disassemble. Even if the story is apocryphal, it's a perfect metaphor for describing the scientific foundations of molecular biology and the largely hidden but deeply flawed assumptions underlying genetic engineering.

The principal presumption behind genetic engineering is the idea that DNA is the "secret to life" and that there is a linear relationship between a gene and a trait. Dr. Richard Strohman, emeritus professor of molecular and cell biology at Berkeley, says that this notion has been discredited. Strohman, one of the most knowledgeable scientists in the field, minces no words when he says that "DNA is most definitely not the secret to life." He explains that, in fact, "the idea that there is a direct relationship between a single gene and a single trait is completely erroneous." He calls this idea "the myth of genetic determinism."

Harvard evolutionary biologist Richard Lewontin agrees, saying that "the entire body of modern science rests on Descartes' metaphor of the world as a machine." The idea that life is a machine, that genetic information flows in a linear fashion, and that DNA accounts for all of an organism's traits is known as the central dogma of molecular biology. "This dogma," says Queens College biologist Barry Commoner, "is, unhappily, false." Geneticist Mae-Wan Ho describes the central dogma as "too simple." It does not take into account environmental influences and the networked communications going on within the genome. The genome, she says, is very dynamic, fluid, and interactive. "What is so disturbing" about these myths, says Lewontin, is that "every biologist knows they are false." Exactly right, says Dr. Strohman, and he goes on to make the most salient point, which is that these false beliefs distort our knowledge. Now, he says, "If we fail to ask the challenging questions, where will the science be when we need it?"

It may be that the mechanistic approach contained in the central dogma persists precisely because it is so simple. Much of life on earth shares a remarkable amount of the genetic code. Once biology moved out of the field and into the laboratory, the rearrangement of molecules seemed to make sense. High-speed computers and the reduction of molecules to data meant that at this level, life seems to be made of interchangeable parts. Apparently genetically modified plants do what they were designed to do, and some say that this is evidence that genetic engineering technology is manageable. Is it?

My search for an answer to that question led me to another building on the Berkeley campus, Hilgard Hall. One of the most beautiful buildings on campus, Hilgard sits by herself like a dignified old lady on the top of a grassy knoll, aging but still graceful. Hilgard, built in 1918, is an architectural celebration of California's rich agricultural past. Her three-story façade is expansively decorated with detailed Florentine Renaissance friezes depicting sheaves of wheat, beehives, swollen bunches of grapes, and overflowing cornucopias. Over the windows are bas-relief sculptures of cows' heads surrounded with wreaths of fruit.

Hilgard Hall was built at a time when mastering the classical form was still important, perhaps even integral, to the function of a building. She continues to hold her ground in the middle of all the robust modern buildings that have risen up around her, standing at a respectful distance. The massive front doors, capped with a giant basket of fruit, open into a cavernous two-story granite entrance hall and a neglected interior. The hallways are dark and dusty, cramped with discarded furniture and filing cabinets. A worn marble staircase leads to the upper floors. In an old laboratory that looks like a museum exhibit on the science of the past, there is an old wooden bench strewn with beakers and rubber hoses. Under the bench, in a wooden drawer, is a plain manila folder, which I was shown. In that folder was a photograph no one's supposed to see. It depicts something that no one is even supposed to know exists. It's a picture of a macabre and distorted corncob. This is not a freak of nature, nor was it created by modern agriculture.

The photograph shows an ear of corn that apparently started growing normally, then turned into another part of the corn plant, then returned to forming kernels, then went back to another form, twisting back and forth, as if it could not make up its mind about what it was. It was produced by the same recombinant DNA technology that is used to create the genetically modified foods that are in our grocery stores today.

This sorry corncob is part of a collection of biological curiosities put together by someone who works in a secure biotechnology research facility. The collection is kept in a plastic bin called "the monster box." Locked inside are some of agricultural biotechnology's dirtiest little secrets. The photograph is disturbing for two reasons: first for what it says about the process used to genetically engineer plants, and second because the owner of the photograph refused to let it be published and asked for anonymity, for fear of retaliation and persecution by the biotechnology industry. The industry is adamant that its processes and products are safe and says that anyone who disagrees is relying on emotion, not science. And yet the industry has not put forward scientific studies that validate its position, and it has a well-deserved reputation for trying to suppress the work of its critics.

This corncob is a mute challenge to industry's claim that recombinant DNA engineering is precise and predictable. The monster box reveals the deeper deceit, the more persistent and dangerous delusion that genetic engineering is based on knowledge of the secret of life. What the monster box, and the fact that evidence of it has to be kept hidden, tells us is that even as we are giving genetic engineering an unprecedented role in the creation of new life on earth, we still have not come to terms with the fact that this technology is fundamentally flawed.

What We Don't Know Can Hurt Us

The U.S. National Academy of Sciences says that the current system of approving GMOs might not detect "unintended changes" in their composition, noting that the process itself could lead to unpredictable consequences. The regulatory agencies, as already noted, ignore the way GMOs are produced, even though there is now enough evidence to show that the process itself is a problem.

Few people know how haphazard the genetic engineering process is, but understanding this is essential in order to evaluate its risks and usefulness fairly. The only precise part of the technique is the selection and modification of the genes to be inserted. To make GMO seeds, you begin by selecting a plant, most likely a patented variety you already own. Then you acquire some new DNA from another organism. These days you can order it online. That DNA is engineered and combined with other genetic constructs and put into a "cassette." This cassette contains the entire complement of genes used to engineer a plant, including the trait genes, viral promoters, genetic switches, and bacterial markers all needed to complete the transformation process. After the creation of the cassette, any illusion of precision ends. The next stage of this process shouldn't be called engineering, in the sense of constructing something according to a plan. What the successful genetic transformation of plants depends on is not design but random luck.

The cassette is inserted into the cells of the target plant. No one knows where it ends up or what happens at the point of insertion. Thousands of insertions are made. All the plants that mutate or fail to grow properly are tossed out. Only those that survive the insertion process and that appear normal are grown out. It's all a matter of looking for those few happy accidents that survive and behave as intended. If one is found, it's cloned, grown out, and becomes the proud parent of a new GMO.

This complicated, time-consuming process is very expensive. The Land Institute of Salina, Kansas, reported on a comparison study of biotech and traditional plant-breeding methods that said "transgenic technology isn't all it's cracked up to be" as a plant-breeding technique, because although the time it takes to develop new hybrids all the way through field testing is roughly the same, the costs of genetic engineering "vastly exceed those of breeding through sexual hybridization." The study showed that the old-fashioned way to develop a new plant variety cost $52,000, while the transgenic method cost $1,301,200. New streamlined methods and marker-assisted breeding techniques are changing these costs and providing other efficiencies, but the process still relies on luck and on some fairly primitive techniques, and is comparatively very expensive.

When genetic engineering was first developed, researchers had a hard time figuring out how to get alien DNA into plant cells without destroying them. For some plants, like tobacco and soybeans, the problem was solved by the use of stealth. A special bacterium called *Agrobacterium* was used to "infect" wounded plant cells and transfer the new DNA inside. But *Agrobacterium* did not work with corn. In the end, that problem was solved by the use of brute force.

Corn put up a remarkable resistance to being genetically engineered. In the mid-1980s, when all the big agrochemical seed companies were betting the farm on biotechnology, corn became the Holy Grail of agricultural genetic engineering. Corn is so fundamental to food and farming in the United States that if it could not be genetically engineered, the technology would not be a commercial success. The way corn was eventually engineered reveals a lot about the flawed methods used in this technology.

This is how it was done. One day in December 1983, on the campus of Cornell University, three men put on booties, gowns, and hair coverings, picked up a gun, and entered the National Submicron Facility, where the university's expensive ion beam accelerators were kept. Once inside, they proceeded to shoot a bunch of onions to smithereens. John Sanford, a plant breeder at Cornell, and his colleagues had spent years looking for ways to speed up the conventional plant-breeding process. Like others, they had difficulty forcing DNA fragments through the relatively thick walls of plant cells, but they thought onions could work because their cells were large enough to withstand the impact.

The idea of using a gun occurred to Sanford while he was waging a backyard battle with some pesky squirrels. He figured out how to load the gun with specially coated beads and then began shooting. Soon pieces of onion were splattered everywhere and the smells of onions and gunpowder permeated the air. It seemed implausible, even laughable, at the time, and to some it still does. But it worked, and the gene gun, which still uses .22-caliber ballistics to shoot DNA into cells, is now a common appliance found in biotechnology laboratories all over the world.

Other "bombardment" tools are used in addition to the gene gun and the *Agrobacterium,* suggesting that a certain degree of violence is inherent in genetic modification. All this is made necessary because plants evolved elaborate defense mechanisms specifically designed to resist just such invasions. Now the suggestion that the problems caused by GMOs, from their health impacts to contamination, might be linked to the process used to create them is gaining credence. Just a few examples of the supporting data now available include:

- a report published in *Nature Biotechnology* finding that the cauliflower mosaic virus, commonly used in GMOs, contains a "recombination hotspot" which makes it unstable and prone to causing mutations, cancer, and new pathogens;
- a peer-reviewed study of scientific literature and USDA documents which found that there is some rearrangement of genes at the site of the insertion and that insertion can cause thousands of mutations and random modifications throughout transgenic plants;
- a study done by the Salk Institute's David Schubert which found that just one transgenic insertion can disrupt 5 percent of the genes in a single-cell bacterium. Translated into plant terms, that means 15,000 to 300,000 genes can get scrambled.

And in 2001, the world's most widely grown GMO, Monsanto's Roundup Ready soybean, was found to contain some mysterious DNA. When that information was brought to Monsanto's attention, the company claimed that the DNA was native to the plant. Later it was shown to be the result of the transformation process.

One report that is causing worldwide concern, given the unexplained massive die-off of bee populations, is the result of a three-year study done in Germany, which found that GMOs had crossed the species barrier from plant pollen into bacteria inside the guts of bees. These GMOs were then found in bees several generations later. This finding worries geneticist Ho, who has been raising the alarm about the unpredictable behavior of GMOs for decades. She says this study provides evidence of horizontal gene transfer, something that used to be considered extremely rare.

Scientists expect genes to stay inside an organism and travel with it "vertically," as when the genes in the food you eat go through the normal processes of digestion and elimination. Now it appears that genes can travel "horizontally," like Casper the Friendly Ghost, moving through the walls of your stomach into other parts of your body. Ho says this is happening because of the genetic engineering process. This process can produce errors such as "insertion mutagenesis and carcinogenesis," genome rearrangement, the activation of dormant viruses, abnormal growths, and metabolic disorders. In 2003, Ho reported on five commercially approved GMOs where the insertion points were unintentionally scrambled or rearranged.

We are just beginning to realize that DNA is not the only, or even perhaps the most significant, player. RNA and gene silencing are also important to the way molecules function. The recent scientific discovery of gene silencing—the ability of genes to turn functions on and off—was, perhaps ironically, first found in transgenic plants. It was thought to be a result of the instability of the genetic engineering process. This key scientific insight is being disregarded by industry and government regulators. Dr. Michael Hansen did an informal survey of more than thirty companies involved in manufacturing transgenic crops and found that they had all observed some level of "transgene inactivation" (gene silencing) in their work. But, Hansen points out, this information has never made it into the scientific literature.

The flawed science and haphazard methods behind genetic engineering may be the great untold story of the twentieth century. There are two explanations for why this story may be so poorly understood and underreported. One is that the nation's scientific literacy is appallingly low. Dr. Jon Miller, a political scientist at Northwestern University, says about 20 to 25 percent of Americans are scientifically savvy, but the rest "don't have a clue," and that has an impact on our effectiveness as citizens. The National Science Foundation says that 70 percent of Americans don't understand basic science, a fact that prompted one late-night talk-show host to quip, "And the other thirty percent don't even know what seventy percent means."

The other reason we don't know what we need to know is that science itself is under attack. Under the Bush administration, scientific reports have been censored, findings distorted, panels disbanded, websites revised, and scientists silenced. The UCS says that 60 percent of the scientists it recently surveyed had personally experienced efforts to suppress their work. Science is more politicized than ever, it seems, or at least since the days of Galileo.

The Best Science Money Can Buy

In February 2007, controversy erupted again on the Berkeley campus. This time the university announced an even more astounding deal with industry: British Petroleum, now known as BP (or Beyond Petroleum), is giving the university $400 million, earmarked for research and development of oil replacements using new technologies. BP is requiring the university to defend the agreement publicly and to pay "significant attention to the evolving regulatory and societal response to genetically modified organisms."

The BP money will add another edifice to the university's burgeoning metropolis of molecular biology. It will also inflate our expectations about what technology can do to solve our energy problems. BP will be using biotechnology and nanotechnology, but its core technology will be synthetic biology, sometimes called "genetic engineering on steroids." Synthetic biology is the ability to construct whole new organisms from prefabricated and preprogrammed molecules. This is the next new big thing in biological design. And it has come along just in time, because the wider scientific community was beginning to realize that there were serious flaws behind genetic engineering and that the obituary for biotechnology was about to be written.

An editorial in the June 2006 issue of *Scientific American* said, "Thirty-three years after the invention of gene-splicing, the reality of biotechnology is still far short of what many once dreamed it would be, partly because the tools for manipulating genes have been crude." Then, without pause or apology, the next sentence reads, "That is about to change." The editorial went on to say that the new technology, synthetic biology, is still embryonic. It warned scientists not to make the same mistakes they made with biotechnology, such as underestimating safety concerns and patenting so indiscriminately that they strangle the life out of their technological baby. As usual, the editorial heaped on the hype that new technologies always attract, saying that this time there would be "colossal payoffs" for medicine, agriculture, and industry.

The ETC Group, a nongovernmental organization based in Canada and the United States, reports that scientists and industrialists who are behind synthetic biology met on the Berkeley campus in May 2006. They decided among themselves, once again, that they would be self-regulating and would not need government oversight. They explicitly said they wanted to develop an "Asilomar-type" model of self-governance. In response, ETC formed a coalition of thirty-five international scientific, environmental, and biological warfare experts, who promptly called on the Berkeley group to withdraw its declaration of self-governance and join in a wider dialogue about the safety issues involved.

Using computational muscle, nanotechnology, and made-to-order genetic constructs, it is now possible to play God in your basement. Custom-made genes can be purchased online for about $2 a base pair, according to *Wired* magazine. Operators are standing by. The pathogen that caused the 1918 flu pandemic has already been re-created. There is almost a kind of computer-game mentality overshadowing biology today. Gone are the dedicated naturalists and plant breeders who were devoted to strengthening, not dominating, the gifts of nature. Given how powerful these tools are, and given the lack of ethical constraints, as well as the lack of controls and public oversight of these developments, the possibilities for abuse are troubling.

The money and political muscle behind the BP deal raise all the same issues of privatization, distortion of the research agenda, and overemphasis on patents that surrounded the Novartis deal. And one UC faculty member, Professor Ignacio Chapela, who led the opposition to the Novartis deal, is stepping forward to oppose BP. He says he's doing it for the same two reasons—to defend academic freedom and because of the dire need for public-interest science. Chapela has taken on this new controversy even though his role in the Novartis controversy almost cost him his academic career.

Is Freedom Academic?

Chapela is a handsome and popular Mexican-born scientist. He was teaching in UC's College of Natural Resources when the university signed the deal with Novartis. And because he took a principled position against it, he was denied tenure. At the time, in the late 1990s, no one was asking the most obvious and basic questions about how GMO plants behaved in the field. Did transgenes move from genetically altered plants into nearby plants? And if they did, how would they behave? Did this gene movement, called introgression, create a new, third type of plant, and did that plant remain stable or change? Chapela's research into these matters sparked one of the most contentious scientific uproars in recent history.

In 2000, Chapela and a graduate student, David Quist, were working in a remote Zapotec Indian village in the mountains near Oaxaca, Mexico. They became alarmed when they accidentally detected GMOs in the local native corn varieties there. This contamination could not have been caused by cross-pollination, because the planting of transgenic corn was banned in Mexico at the time. Chapela and Quist took more samples and subjected them to more tests when they returned to Berkeley.

They made two astounding findings. The first confirmed the presence of transgenic DNA in the local corn. The second found that those transgenes appeared to be unstable and to have moved around in the genome. The first finding was shocking because the region where they found the transgenes is the birthplace of corn, the place where corn originated and where it has its greatest genetic diversity. If the "center of origin" of corn was pervasively contaminated with GMOs, it would be an environmental disaster. The second finding threatened a sacred tenet of biotechnology: the belief that transgenes are stable and behave predictably.

If Quist and Chapela's data were validated, it could turn the scientific tide against genetic engineering.

Chapela and Quist were aware of the significance of their work, so they took the precaution of going through the long process of peer review and publication in the journal *Nature*. This is the international gold standard for science, because it means the results are accepted by other scientists and can be used for subsequent research. When a disagreement erupts over a peer-reviewed study, typically it takes the form of a letter to the editor of the journal challenging the research or its methods. That's followed by a back-and-forth exchange between scientists.

What happened to Chapela and Quist was something else altogether. It began in Mexico, before the *Nature* article was published. Chapela says that late one night government officials took him to a deserted office building and heavy-handedly "suggested" that he withhold his research. He refused. Then, after publication, a critique was posted on a little-known website called AgBioWorld. It appeared to be a legitimate assessment of the work, but as the British newspaper the *Guardian* reported later, the posting was actually the work of a public relations firm that had been hired by Monsanto.

Later, when studies in Mexico verified the presence of GMOs there, the scientists involved were told not to talk about their research. Then, in what appears to be an industry-orchestrated attack, scientists began deluging *Nature* with demands that the paper be withdrawn. Critiques came from a former graduate student and members of faculty at Berkeley who had been supporters of the Novartis deal. Under pressure, the editor of *Nature* published a letter that sounded like but wasn't really a retraction of the original paper.

In the end, the uproar revealed two minor errors that Quist and Chapela acknowledged, but their results remained valid. It was all very bizarre, and painful for Chapela and Quist. But apparently it had the desired effect, because many people believe that their findings were rescinded. What made all of this especially difficult for Chapela was the tenure issue. In the spring of

2002, the faculty voted thirty-two to one to grant tenure. That one opposing vote resulted in what another member of the committee later called a "disgraceful," long, and bitter administrative review, which decided against Chapela.

In 2004, Michigan State University published a detailed and comprehensive review of the Cal-Novartis deal. It concluded that "there is little doubt that the UCB-Novartis agreement" played an "unsatisfactory role" in the decision to deny tenure to Chapela. It also found that the agreement was "outside the mainstream for research contracts with industry" and that the university administration, which received one third of the funds, had disregarded its own potential conflict of interest in the deal. For the next few years, Chapela continued teaching and continued standing up for academic freedom. He sued the university and eventually was given full tenure.

Chapela is only one of a growing list of scientists whose work at public institutions is under attack by industry. Dr. John Losey of Cornell University, who revealed the impact of GMO corn pollen on monarch butterflies, suffered a media campaign aimed at discrediting his work. Dr. Arpad Pusztai of the Rowett Institute in Scotland was fired, his files were seized, and a major media campaign was aimed at discrediting him and his work after he found immune and histological damage to rats fed transgenic potatoes. Pusztai was exonerated, but his ordeal was so egregious that Prince Charles said, "The nation owes you an apology." His work was also validated by a recently released study from Russia showing tissue damage in rats fed transgenic potatoes. That study was released only after an eight-year struggle with industry, which sought to suppress it.

Another scientist at Berkeley, Professor Tyrone Hayes, says that Syngenta Corporation interfered with his work. Hayes has been studying the effects of the powerful weed killer Atrazine on frogs and other amphibians for years. He had a research contract with Syngenta, the manufacturer of Atrazine, but when he found that frogs were adversely affected even by very low levels of Atrazine, he says Syngenta tried to prevent him from publishing his results. Eventually Hayes funded the research himself and successfully published his results.

There are about a half-dozen documented instances where researchers have been denied access to transgenic material by companies that do not want them studied. There are reports of rigged crop trials and inadequate and unreliable industry statements to regulators, and many anecdotes about how the biotechnology industry has tried to smear its critics. Professor Krimsky says that because of the way public universities and research institutions have been compromised by private interests, they no longer deserve the public's unquestioning trust. This applies to government science as well. Krimsky told the *New York Times* that the big national science advisory panels have just two rules: one is that a scientist must not have a conflict of interest, and the second is that rule number one can be waived.

Chuck Benbrook is one of the few independent economists who, using publicly available data, has shown that agricultural genetic engineering is not living up to its promises. When I asked him why there aren't more studies like his, he said it was because academics and policy analysts are afraid. "These companies play hardball. They've gotten their way. They've benefited from intimidation and recrimination for so long, it's a culture." For years Benbrook managed a website that published studies relating to agricultural biotechnology. He says the level of suppression going on is "un-freakin'-believable!" He shakes his head at the thought and adds that this problem "exists below the radar screen, like a cancer on the independence of thought. It really bothers me. The level of intellectual dishonesty in the discourse on GM crops, in the name of public institutions, in the name of famous scientists who sign on these position statements who have no clue about what they have agreed to or what's behind it, it's a very sad sign of the times. It's an indicator that we are losing the ability of critically evaluating the choices that we need to make, as a society."

Ignacio Chapela says that the distorted corncob in the monster box is a stand-in for all that science doesn't know about the molecular world. And, he adds, it's a proxy for ourselves, because in a sense, what we do to seeds, we do to ourselves. We have lost our common sense and what Rachel Carson called our "sense of wonder." It seems to me that science, at its best, should stimulate our curiosity rather than pander to the worst of human hubris.

I was sitting on the front steps of Hilgard Hall on a beautiful warm spring day in 2002 thinking about this when I looked downhill at the massive bulk of the Life Science Building and its modern annex. It represents the swelled expectations for science in the mid-twentieth century. To my right, on the leading edge of campus, was Koshland Hall, representing the more upscale late-twentieth-century ideal of molecular biology. Behind me, in the distant hills, were the laboratories that BP will be using, supposedly to save us from our prior engineering excesses. And right where I sat was a building that represents all the hopes and dreams of the agrarian ideal, carved in stone. Above the entrance to Hilgard, massive Roman letters declare the purpose of the building: TO RESCUE FOR HUMAN SOCIETY THE NATIVE VALUES OF RURAL LIFE.

These are the choices we made in the twentieth century. These are the investments we, the public, made in the intellectual infrastructure for agriculture. Hilgard Hall was named for Eugene Hilgard, a former dean of the College of Agriculture. He was a highly respected scientist who compiled the first database of California's soils. For most of the twentieth century, science combined respect for the natural world with research in the service of humanity. This wasn't a sentimental value; it was the legal mandate for all land-grant colleges. They were given land by the federal government to fund their mission, along with the charge that they "promote a sound and prosperous agriculture and rural life as indispensable to . . . national prosperity and security." And they were part of the nineteenth-century ideal that an educated citizenry was essential to democracy.

The privatization of public institutions and the politicization of science are a purposeful strategy on the part of those who believe that private technology should be given the mandate to solve all our problems. Erwin Chargaff too was concerned about the direction the science he loved was taking. In 1976 he wrote, "My life has been marked by two immense and fateful scientific discoveries: the splitting of the atom and the recognition of the chemistry of heredity and its subsequent manipulation. It is the mistreatment of nucleus that, in both instances, lies at the basis: the nucleus of the atom, the nucleus of the cell. In both instances do I have the feeling that science has transgressed a barrier that should have remained inviolate. As happens often in science, the first discoveries were made by thoroughly admirable men, but the crowd that came right after had a more mephitic smell."

FOUR

The Ownership Society

> This is the patent age of new inventions
> for killing bodies, and for saving souls,
> All propagated with the best intentions.
>
> LORD BYRON

America's Heartland

America's heartland is not so much a place as it is an idea. It's an image that runs deep in the nation's psyche. The visual stereotype that goes with it is a cloudless blue sky, a bright red barn, and amber waves of grain. Sometimes there's an old tractor puttering through the fields. The emotion this image evokes is admiration for the independent farmer and respect for America's rural communities. Just cue up a few chords of fiddle music and you have a theme used by every politician who ever ran for national office. It's a staple image used by agribusiness in its advertising as well. It can be found all over the grocery store, especially on boxes of cereal, put there to suggest that the food you're buying comes from a farm rather than from a factory.

The reality is that the life of the farmer today is all but forgotten. Farmers have been living under harsh economic conditions for the past three decades, a chronic crisis of falling incomes and rising costs. The pain of these challenges was documented by Joel Dyer in his book *Harvest of Rage.* He explained how the financial losses for farm families were so unbearable that suicide became the number-one cause of death on America's farms. These economic equations may change as the growing biofuels industry drives up the price of commodities, but there are no guarantees that this will correct the long-term economic slump. The only sector of the agricultural economy making any money is agribusiness, and those companies are positioning themselves to be the beneficiaries of the biofuels boom as well.

Recent polls throughout the Midwest report that the primary concern of farmers these days is corporate concentration. If there is any one thing that brings the myth and the reality of the heartland into sharp contrast, it's the increasingly small number of players at the top and the increasingly dire straits of farmers at the bottom. Agribusiness is now controlled by a handful of agrochemical/seed/pharmaceutical companies. They are highly integrated and interrelated, meaning that just a few companies own or control the seed, farm inputs, shipping and transportation, mills, and processing. They manufacture the animal feed that consumes more than half of our grain production and use the other half for the products we eat and their related industries. The problem is, with control of agriculture in just a few hands, farmers are no longer autonomous, and they can get trapped in a system that often brings them to ruin. Just ask Kem Ralph, a cotton farmer in Tennessee, what he thinks it really means to be a farmer in America's heartland today.

Having a conversation with Ralph is like tasting a spoonful of thick sorghum syrup. His southern drawl has a smooth and sweet cadence, with slightly bitter overtones. The taste of his story lingers too. It's complex, but in many ways it exemplifies the personal torment and outrage that other farmers have felt about what is going on. Ralph and his brother grow cotton on land their father began farming in 1937. Over the past six years, Ralph has been through a series of civil trials that have been emotionally wrenching and financially devastating. He was sued by Monsanto, has endured false accusations and betrayal by other farmers, and has been fined almost $3 million. As things progressed, he got really angry at Monsanto and burned the seed that was going to be used as evidence against him. Lying about that landed him in prison for four months. By 2007, he was almost completely ruined and had to file for bankruptcy.

It all began, Ralph said, when he ran out of cotton seed a few years back. He went to a seed dealer, who said all that was left was some GMO cotton seed another farmer had returned. So Ralph bought it. Nothing was said about signing any agreement. Ordinarily Monsanto requires farmers who buy its patented GMO seed to sign a contract called a technology use agreement. These contracts allow Monsanto to go onto private land and investigate the farmer's records and practices. They bind the farmer to Monsanto's products for several years, tell the farmer how to plant, and require the farmer to use only Monsanto's chemicals. Farmers can use seed for only a single season and may not reuse, sell, or replant seed after harvest. All farmers who use GMO seed are exposed to enormous legal liabilities, because Monsanto strictly enforces all of its rights.

According to a 2005 study conducted by the Center for Food Safety (CFS), Monsanto has an annual budget of $10 million and a staff of seventy-five devoted exclusively to investigating and prosecuting farmers. Some farmers, like Ralph, have been sued by Monsanto even though they did not sign an agreement. Monsanto says that Ralph signed an agreement. Ralph says the signature on the agreement was a forgery. This argument is not uncommon. The CFS reports that forging farmers' signatures on these agreements "is called common by seed dealers. Nearly one in 10 of Monsanto's lawsuits involved such forgeries."

The report by the CFS, *Monsanto vs. U.S. Farmers,* is full of shocking and tragic stories of farmers caught in the crossfire of contract terms they never agreed to and Monsanto's vicious and intrusive tactics. Farmers have been sued when their crops have been contaminated by Monsanto's seed or when GMO plants came up on their land as volunteers. "In all of these cases," says the CFS, "because of the way patent law has been applied, farmers are technically liable." Monsanto has set up hotlines and taken out radio ads encouraging farmers to inform on one another.

They get about five hundred tips a year. Ralph's problems began with just such an anonymous tip, a practice he calls "downright un-American." The CFS says, "No farmer is safe from the long reach of Monsanto."

Monsanto also uses private police and hires Pinkerton investigators to find evidence against any farmers it suspects of infringing on its intellectual property rights. Mitchell Scruggs, a cotton farmer in Mississippi who was sued by Monsanto, says that the company "hired the whole city of Tupelo's night police force. They bought a lot across the street from me for surveillance. They're spending all this money on airplanes, helicopters, detectives, and lawyers. They want to destroy me to show others what could happen to them." It does appear that these tactics are intended to frighten farmers. Monsanto's lawyers showed up in criminal court when Ralph was being sentenced and told the judge that he should be sent to jail as an example to other farmers. Scruggs says, "It's a God-given right that farmers were given when they were born to save these seeds. All we are is farmers trying to scrape a living out of this dirt."

Monsanto has the right to enforce its contracts and patents. It says that if it doesn't strictly enforce its rights, farmers will get away with reusing seed and Monsanto will lose money. However, the tactics the company uses go beyond the norms of enforcing the terms of ordinary commercial transactions. Basically, the farmer is presented with "evidence" of something "illegal" and told to pay a fine or face a lawsuit. The law firms Monsanto uses to sue farmers are careful about how they word their letters, but from the farmer's point of view, getting a letter like that is intimidating. What farmer has the financial means and stamina to take on a corporation like Monsanto?

To date, the number of farmers investigated by Monsanto's agents is in the thousands. Many of them get threatening letters. And the number of farmers ending up in litigation is growing. CFS says that by the end of 2005, Monsanto had brought cases against 351 farmers and 47 small businesses or farm companies in 27 different states and had been awarded judgments amounting to a total of $16,849,255.07 from these patent cases. Rodney Nelson, a North Dakota farmer who was sued by Monsanto, says, "It's hard enough to farm as it is. You don't need a big seed supplier like Monsanto trying to trip you up and then chasing you down with lawyers."

In the end, most cases settle out of court, but even so, CFS says some settlements are coerced. And when farmers do settle, they are effectively silenced, because they have to sign confidentiality agreements that forbid them to discuss their cases. If the farmers litigate and lose, they have to pay not only their own expenses but Monsanto's costs and attorneys' fees as well. And some, like Ralph, even have to pay the costs of being investigated as well as punitive damages.

Some farmers are fighting back. The poster boy of Monsanto seed-patent litigation is the courageous and long-suffering Canadian farmer Percy Schmeiser. Schmeiser's case was one of the first and best-known because he refused to let Monsanto bully him. His canola fields were contaminated with Monsanto's GMO canola. Since he had been a seed dealer and breeder, he could prove he had not purchased or planted GMO seed. However, Monsanto relentlessly investigated and sued him and he was financially ruined by years of litigation. Ultimately the Canadian courts sided with Monsanto, saying that it didn't matter how Monsanto's genes got into Schmeiser's fields; once they were there, the patents could be enforced.

Schmeiser has pledged to do what it takes to stop Monsanto from doing what it did to him to other farmers. Farmers in both the United States and Canada are continuing their crusade to stop Monsanto's contamination suits and to ask the courts to protect their right to save seeds. There are class action and antitrust lawsuits against Monsanto for price fixing and seed monopolizing, but so far the courts have ruled in favor of Monsanto. Given the way patent law works, the only hope for a remedy may be legislation. Scruggs says that Monsanto now owns so much of the seed industry and the seed companies are so bound up with each other, it can charge whatever it wants or prosecute whomever it pleases.

He says, "It's destroying this country to let a big corporation control all the food and fiber through the seed."

Why would farmers bother with GMO seed if it carries such high environmental and legal risks? Because, Ralph says, "Farmers are addicted to it," and "it's easy." The economics of commodity farming leave many farmers with no choice, even though they understand that this seed increases the control that industry has and thus the prices the industry can charge. Ralph says, "I'm not worried about the $2.9 million in damages against me. I'm worried about the rights of people getting charged such tremendous amounts for seed." He added that because of this control over patented seed, farmers are throwing away millions of tons of seed every year, because they cannot replant it or sell it. "What a waste," he said "and sister, it's all because they want to control our food!"

Farmers like Ralph can't be blamed for feeling hurt and angry. At the end of all the messages he leaves on my answering machine, in a voice tinged with pain, Ralph always calls me "sister" and always thanks me kindly for listening to his story. Then he ends by saying, "But you know, sister, our justice system just sucks."

Life: Patent Pending

As the nation was being founded, there was much discussion about where to locate the capital city. Some wanted it to be New York City or Philadelphia; others wanted it closer to the plantations of the South. Our "founding farmers" prevailed, and a city was built on a swamp near the Potomac River. Even given its obvious political importance and its magnificent architecture, Washington, D.C., retains the characteristics of its original nature as a quagmire. American corporations, particularly Monsanto, seem to have mastered the skills of navigating this bog better than most. Certainly the farmers being sued by Monsanto have not found any help there. So far the White House, Congress, and the Supreme Court have all taken Monsanto's side.

There are historical reasons for this. Patents are an extension of our long-standing love affair with private property rights, a founding principle of our system of government. Enforcing these rights, however, is often more like the old maxim of the Wild West that says whoever gets to the sheriff's office first wins. It used to be that whoever got to the patent office first won the patent as well. Now, whoever gets hold of the power in Washington first prevails.

The original Patent Office in Washington was easy to find. It was the third building constructed for the government there, after the White House and the Capitol. It's a beautiful replica of the Parthenon, graced with a portico of Doric columns and designed, as architectural historian Paul Hogarth says, as "a temple to Power through Knowledge." The building, now the National Portrait Gallery, is one of the best remaining works of Greek Revival architecture in America. Walt Whitman worked there as a clerk for the Bureau of Indian Affairs and as a volunteer nurse during the Civil War.

Eventually the Patent and Trademark Office (PTO) moved to much larger and less historically interesting quarters across the river in Virginia. There employees sort through all the applications and award patents, which, President Lincoln famously said, add "the fuel of interest to the fire of genius." The basic idea is that the public gains when the government supports science and invention. A patent is a government grant giving someone exclusive rights over an "invention" for a limited period of time.

What can be patented, how long the patent is good for, and the rights of inventors and challengers have been broadly expanded over the years. It used to be that an invention had to be something useful, but it could not be obvious, a product of nature, or a "mere method of doing business." Now patenting has become its own wealth-creation mechanism, and it's used to protect, and thus generate income from, just about everything. Ideas and methods can be patented. Until recently it was always understood that works of nature like seeds and sexually reproducing plants would not be patentable. That too has now changed.

How seeds became patentable private property is a remarkable story. For almost a century, the USDA distributed high-quality seeds for free to farmers and gardeners throughout the country. Seeds were saved and traded locally. When hybrid corn seed became popular, between the world wars, farmers began buying their seed from private companies. As the seed industry grew, it began its own plant-breeding programs, and unlike government plant breeders, private breeders wanted to protect their proprietary interests.

The legal framework began to shift toward patenting in the 1930s, with the passage of the Plant Patent Act (PPA). It was the first time breeders could get monopoly ownership over their plants, and it stimulated the private plant-breeding business. The PPA applied only to asexually reproducing plants, like grafted roses and fruit trees. Sexually reproducing plants and seeds, as well as some asexually propagated crops, like potatoes, were not covered by these plant patents because they were considered vital to the nation's economy.

Then, in 1970, Congress passed the Plant Variety Protection Act (PVPA), which expanded intellectual property rights over a variety of sexually reproducing plants. Breeders were given certificates, issued by the USDA, granting them exclusive rights for up to twenty-five years. But the law preserved important exemptions for researchers and farmers, who were allowed to save and reuse seed. Although these certificates were called "plant patents," they were not the kind of patents the PTO issues for contraptions. Those are called "utility patents," and they are governed by very different laws. As the biotechnology industry got into the plant-breeding business, it was not content with PPA patents; it wanted the control and ownership rights that utility patents would give it.

More Heartbreak in the Heartland

During the 1980s two important trends converged that would dramatically change the lives of American farmers. On the biological level, genetic engineering was gaining dominance, and on the legal front there was a coordinated effort to develop a new international system for protecting the intellectual property rights of plant breeders. The first step was taken when the International Union for the Protection of New Varieties of Plants (known as UPOV) was adopted. Until then, the time-honored and legally sanctioned practice had been that farmers everywhere could freely save and exchange seed. Almost one and a half billion people worldwide were, and still are, dependent on the seed saving of small farmers for their food security.

In the early 1990s, some changes were made to UPOV that at first glance seem reasonable. Signatory countries were told that they could either accept new uniform rules governing patents or come up with their own patent system. This tactic is called "harmonizing" trade-related intellectual property rights, and it gives technology companies access to world markets. (It suits the interests of software developers as well.) In theory this appears to offer nations a choice. But in practice it is a forced choice, and it creates an opening for agribusiness and biotechnology interests to move in and influence the process on the national and international levels. As a result, domestic and international laws substantially expanded the ownership rights of companies and curtailed the rights of farmers.

The next steps for the seed and biotechnology industry were to get the United States to join the UPOV convention and then amend U.S. law, the PVPA, to comply with its rules. At the same time, plant breeders began applying to the PTO to get utility patents on sexually reproducing plants. Together, these strategies laid the groundwork for the lawsuits the biotechnology companies would soon bring against farmers over seed-patent infringement.

Congress never authorized the PTO to issue utility patents on seeds, although it had the opportunity to do so in 1994, when it amended the PVPA. By this time the conflict between the seed companies and the farmers was coming to a head. Both sides showed up in force at the hearings. The farmer seed savers were represented by Becky Winterboer, an Iowa farmer who was there to literally beg Congress to maintain the legal exemption in the PVPA that allowed farmers to save seed.

The Winterboers, like small farmers all across the heartland, had developed their own seed that was adapted to local conditions. They also sold it to their neighbors, a time-honored practice in farm country. Then, in 1991, the Asgrow Seed Company, now owned by the giant Upjohn Corporation, sued the Winterboers, claiming that their seed sales violated the PVPA. Asgrow claimed that some of the Winterboer crop originally came from Asgrow's varieties. This was not a patent infringement case; it was a direct challenge to the rights of farmers to save and sell seed under the PVPA. Although the lawsuit was an emotional and financial nightmare for the Winterboers, the federal court of appeals ruled in their favor. At the time of the congressional hearing, however, the appeal Asgrow had taken to the U.S. Supreme Court was still pending.

Also speaking on behalf of farmers was Hope Shand, then director of the Rural Advancement Foundation International (RAFI), a nonprofit group dedicated to the preservation of family farms and the conservation of genetic diversity. Shand put the importance of farmer-saved seed in context. Crop genetic diversity, she said, is essential to the stability of the food supply and the livelihood of farmers. Farmers are the first line of defense against the loss of that diversity. Farmers who save and replant seeds develop resistant and locally adapted strains. Furthermore, Shand pointed out, every major crop grown in the United States—corn, soybeans, rice, cotton, potatoes, and wheat—originally came from somewhere else. Our seeds were originally bred by farmers in other countries. Awarding exclusive rights to these varieties to seed companies would effectively and unfairly deprive farmers in developing nations of their rightful heritage and narrow the genetic diversity of these important crops.

The seed industry's position was that the farmers' exemption eroded its profits. It didn't present direct evidence of that claim. Instead it complained about how farmers were "brown bagging," that is, reselling seeds grown from privately developed varieties. Shand agreed that brown bagging was a problem, but whether it was legal or not, she and representatives of other farm groups questioned just how much it actually harmed commercial seed sales. USDA data showed that farmers had spent almost $4 billion on purchased seed the year before the hearings, in 1992. The USDA testified that farmer seed trading made a crucial difference to the farmer on an individual basis and said it was important for farmers to retain the choice to save seed.

In the end, Congress amended the PVPA to expand the rights of the industry and restrict the rights of farmers, but it did not entirely eliminate the farmer seed-saving exemption. Then the Supreme Court ruled in the Asgrow case, further restricting farmers' rights. All that was left for the farmers was the right to save seed for replanting as a crop or to use as food. Farmers and local informal breeders were effectively put out of the seed business. It's hard to imagine now, but it wasn't all that long ago—less than fifteen years—that farmers in America still had the right to reuse their seed the way they wanted.

Patently Obvious

During the last two decades of the twentieth century, the Supreme Court, Congress, and the PTO made changes that eventually led to the granting of utility patents on seeds. It began with a U.S. Supreme Court decision in 1980 that upheld a patent on a tiny genetically engineered organism. It was a five–four split decision, which means that one justice in one case tipped the balance of power toward the privatization of life. That decision also brought about a profound social transformation. It opened the door to the patenting of every imaginable living thing. Twenty percent of the DNA in the human body is now patented. Many of the genes in your body are already owned by someone else, most likely a pharmaceutical company or an institution. The regents of the University of California, for instance, own eighty-nine human genes.

Corporations like DuPont, Dow, and Monsanto say they have to have patents in order to ensure the profits they want and attract the investment they need. But patents also help control the market for their products. The industry has been busy rearranging and reinventing fats, sugars, proteins, and other nutrients, searching for something nutritious to offer that's not already available to anyone eating a balanced diet. Its GMO spud was a dud, the tomato rotted, and the papaya stinks.

My favorite example is omega-3-enhanced foods. Omega-3 is an important nutrient that can be deficient in the industrial diet, so adding it to common foods seems like a good idea. The easy way to do this is to put some flaxseed on your cereal, but never mind. The food industry needs a product to sell. So to get eggs with more omega-3 fatty acids in them, you can feed chickens a vegetarian diet high in flaxseed and other sources of omega-3. Or you can genetically engineer the chicken to produce these enhanced eggs. Now, why would anyone bother genetically engineering something when it's obviously easy to accomplish the same thing in a much easier and cheaper way? The answer is, by using biotechnology you can alter something at its molecular level and then you can patent it.

Patents are the lifeblood of biotechnology. They allow the agrochemical companies to control their products' place in the stream of commerce. Patenting seeds, then, is a key part of the GMO industry's strategy to control the market. Patents enable industry to make money even when its products are not particularly useful or necessary, because when a monopoly right has been granted, the product has built-in scarcity and thus economic value. The bottom line for the technology is that its only use is to create products; it cannot be, and has not been, used to solve real problems. For consumers, the industry has yet to come up with a product that is not already available without using biotechnology. For farmers, GMOs only work as a substitute for chemicals or expensive labor. As of now, genetic engineering is an invention in search of a necessity.

Still, the seed companies were not secure in their patenting strategy. Congress had considered the matter but consistently rejected the option of applying utility patents to seed and reinforced the use of plants' patent-like protections under the PVPA. And there had always been the possibility that someone would challenge patents on living things in court. The seed industry wanted to remove any lingering legal questions about its patents. It got its chance in 1998, when Pioneer Hi-Bred, which held seventeen patents on corn, brought a patent infringement action against a small seed dealer in Iowa called Farm Advantage. The question in the case was, were the utility patents on seeds that had been issued by the PTO valid, or did Congress intend for the PVPA to govern sexually reproducing plants and seeds exclusively?

This question was so important that the case was fast-tracked to the U.S. Supreme Court. Farm Advantage and a few other small seed dealers, along with farmers' right groups, submitted briefs against the industrial patenting of seed. The entire biotechnology industry, the international seed industry, the federal government, the PTO, and the Justice Department argued for the validity of the utility patents. By this time the U.S. government was firmly on the side of the biotechnology industry and had long since stopped acting in the interests of American farmers when it came to seeds and plant breeding.

On December 10, 2001, the Supreme Court held that utility patents could be used for seeds and plants. The opinion of the Court was written by Justice Clarence Thomas, who had been a lawyer for Monsanto. And while his former employer stood to gain enormously from this action, technically Thomas did not have a conflict of interest, because Monsanto was not a party to the lawsuit. He could have recused himself but did not.

License to Kill

Believe it or not, the biotechnology industry finds all the effort and expense it has to expend enforcing its seed patents to be burdensome. Suing American farmers is nothing compared to what it would take for these companies to investigate and force farmers in other countries to obey all their contract provisions. Their dream solution would be to find some way to protect seed patents wherever they are used without law enforcement. And while biotechnology companies do not seem to be concerned about the impact that their GMO contamination has on the public or the environment, they do worry that farmers might someday successfully sue them for damages. The answer to both problems appeared with the invention of the "terminator technologies."

Terminators are a form of biological patent enforcement. One method works by engineering seed so it does not germinate after producing a single crop. Another works by keeping the seed from germinating until it is doused with a proprietary chemical. Others, often called "traitor technologies," use chemicals like antibiotics to turn traits off or on. These suicide seeds have been developed for use in crops grown in third world countries, to prevent farmers there from reusing seed.

The name terminator was given to these technologies by the ETC Group, which says that dozens of patents have been issued for various versions. The European version is a chemically activated seed killer called the "verminator" because it uses rat genes to switch on the delayed seed death. These genetic controls were first developed and patented jointly by the largest cotton seed dealer in the world, Delta and Pine Land (D&PL) of Scott, Mississippi, and the largest agricultural concern in the world, the United States Department of Agriculture. When the USDA's work on terminators came to light, the department defended its role, saying that public investment in these technologies was justified because they would "increase the value of proprietary seed owned by US seed companies and open up new markets in the Second and Third World countries."

The promoters of terminator technologies call the idea a "technology protection system." They say it will protect plants from being contaminated by transgenes and benefit farmers. According to D&PL's brochure, in 1996, when GMO cotton was first being introduced, farmers in the Texas High Plains saved their own seed. Only 10 percent of land there was planted with purchased seed. Just a few years later, 90 percent of the seed planted there was purchased. "Obviously," the brochure says, "farmers have been the beneficiaries of [this] new technology." It goes on to say that if terminators were used everywhere, U.S. farmers, who now pay extra for patented seeds, would not have to "compete unfairly" with farmers in other countries, who don't buy patented seeds. This makes sense, Shand says, because the important point to understand about terminators is that they're not designed to enhance life or to improve agriculture. They have only one purpose: to force farmers to buy patented seeds.

D&PL claims that its product uses "an environmentally safe treatment" which is applied "prior to the sale of the seed... At the time of germination, [it] will trigger an irreversible series of events rendering the seed produced on farmers' plants non-viable for re-planting." It does not mention all the other genetic constructs that were included in the GMO, such as viral vectors, repressors, and promoters that could be affected by the switching system, and it does not say that the chemical used to trigger the effect is the antibiotic tetracycline. The way it works is that the genes wait and let the plant grow normally, and then, just as the seed reaches maturity, they send a signal to generate a toxin that kills the seeds' reproductive capacity. The seed can be used as grain, but it cannot be used as seed because it will not germinate. Another name for this idea might be "sleeper cell" seeds.

The timing of the process is the tricky part. Canadian geneticist Joe Cummins says that some terminators contain genes that use toxins derived from diphtheria that digest cellular RNA and others use excess hormone production to abort the seed embryo. The seed perceives itself as a foreign invader and self-destructs. What should worry us, he says, is not just that these sterility traits are bred into the seeds, but that these crops will be consumed by birds and insects and will cross-pollinate with other plants. Shand says they will have an impact on whatever they come into contact with as well. She says that although the inventors vehemently deny it, the terminator genes can get out. "If pollen from a terminator corn plant hitches a ride on the wind or an insect and gets into nonterminator corn, it could transfer its sterility trait to the neighboring corn plant. If we have learned anything from agricultural biotechnology, it's that genes get around." These seeds have completely novel, unknown, and possibly allergenic or toxic properties. Plus their timing apparatus might not work perfectly, so that the toxins could be released early, killing the plant. And in this case, when the toxic gene gets into the environment, it will act as the biological equivalent of the police state, with a license to kill.

The U.S. Forest Service has tested transgenic poplar trees in Oregon that use suicide cells to eliminate flowering. There has been a flood of patent applications for terminator-like genetic control of sexual development in seeds, trees, and crops. Scientists who are opposed to terminator technologies have pointed out that as yet there is no proof that they work. Meanwhile, worldwide opposition to terminator technologies continues to grow. Over five hundred organizations, including many academic and research institutions as well as farmer groups, are calling for a ban. At the UN Convention on Biological Diversity meeting in March 2006, delegates reaffirmed the international moratorium on terminator field testing and commercialization.

Monsanto publicly renounced terminator technologies in 1999, saying that it understood that "there is something psychologically offensive about sterile seeds in every culture." In a 2006 e-mail message, Monsanto told the ETC Group that it stands by its pledge "not to commercialize sterile seed technologies in food crops." The sincerity of this statement, however, should be measured against Monsanto's attempts to buy D&PL. Ever since its first effort failed, Monsanto and D&PL have been embroiled in a $2 billion lawsuit. In 2006, the *Wall Street Journal* reported that Monsanto offered D&PL $600 million to end the lawsuit and consider a new offer. If the acquisition is approved by the Justice Department, Monsanto will gain control of 60 percent of the U.S. cotton seed market.

Seeds, instead of being a source of life, are now becoming a source of death. Forcing a seed to abort its life force is an unnatural and immoral act. The fact that anyone would even think of this, let alone allow it to become a commercial enterprise, is a sign either of just how degraded the field of biotechnology has become or of just how desperate the industry is. The insidiousness of terminator technologies, says biologist Martha Crouch, is that "they weaken the seed cycle, robbing crops of their ability to regenerate without corporate sponsorship. Rather than making our crops more vulnerable, we should be promoting their maximum capabilities, so they can be our full partners in responding to whatever comes our way. In this time of global change, we need strength and vitality. So do our seeds."

The Power of Ideas

A few years back, George W. Bush said, "I love the ownership society," using a term coined by Karl Rove. He said he just liked the *idea* of owning something. That's all ownership is, really; it's just an idea. We made it up, along with all the legal structures and economic values that support it. Private property rights are fundamental to our economic system, and they have extended their reach into every aspect of our lives. Patents have now become "the highest-valued assets in any economy," says an economist at the Organization for Economic Cooperation and Development in Europe. It has gone too far, however, and the overuse of intellectual property rights is stifling innovation.

Recent appellate decisions indicate that the courts are beginning to consider setting boundaries on the use of patents. Public-interest organizations are ramping up their attacks on patenting. The Public Patent Foundation (PUBPAT) has challenged the four patents that Monsanto has been using to sue farmers. Its request for reexamination of the patents has been accepted by the PTO, and PUBPAT says that challenges like this have been successful 70 percent of the time. Joe Mendelson, legal director of the Center for Food Safety, says, "I actually think things are starting to turn around." He points to several cases the center has won lately as well the number of farmers who are fighting Monsanto. Many farmer groups are suing biotechnology companies for damages caused by GMO contamination, and several antitrust actions are pending against Monsanto in the United States and Canada.

Plant breeders often want to share their work and engage in an open exchange of ideas, because that facilitates problem solving and is likely to result in research in the public interest. When research was being conducted openly and in the public interest, it was shared by publication. But now intellectual property rights and patents constrict this activity and limit what is studied. Patents, sociologist Kelly Moore says, reward products, not ideas. In response, researchers frustrated by these trends are finding new ways to share knowledge. In Davis, California, a group called Public Intellectual Property Resource (PIPRA) has the stated goal of ensuring "the broadest applications of existing and emerging agricultural technologies for the development of subsistence crops for developing countries, and specialty crops in developed countries." It encourages universities and nonprofits to broaden the way they manage their intellectual property and have worked with forty institutions and five countries.

BioForge (Biological Information for an Open Society) is working on open research methods in the field of agroecology, using the concept of the commons, which is now understood to include any property (intellectual or real) that is held in common, in the public domain or the public trust. There is the "creative commons," which allows use and distribution of protected material with permission and credit; the creation of a patent commons; the explicit inclusion of local knowledge as part of the restoration of the commons in local communities; and, on a wider scale, the renewal of common property systems by traditional and indigenous farmers. Some groups are also beginning to protect their knowledge by publishing it, putting it in the public domain, or taking out defensive patents. What all this means is that grassroots groups are forcing change from the bottom up.

On the local level, legal restrictions and bans on GMOs have been passed by cities and counties. A California legislator has proposed a bill protecting California farmers from GMO contamination and giving them other rights as well as prohibiting open-field biopharming. Other states have made progress on legislation, although nothing substantial has made it into law yet. And there has been an industry backlash. Most state legislatures favor industry, and some have passed industry-sponsored laws that prohibit local jurisdictions from making their own rules governing GMOs. A national law that would ban states and localities from deciding for themselves how to protect their food system was slipped into the farm bill being considered in Congress in 2007.

Control of the federal government by big business has now reached the point where people no longer expect the government to act on their behalf. They are finding other ways to control their food and farming locally, as people always have. Throughout the history of the world, autocratic efforts to control agriculture have always failed. And in the heartland, people are returning to local food and fuel production and getting support and inspiration from none other than country icon Willie Nelson.

Almost twenty years ago, when Congress passed a farm bill that gave billions in subsidies to the country's richest farmers and left needy farmers in the lurch, Nelson decided to act. He founded Farm Aid, and every year he and other country music luminaries sing at concerts that raise millions to help America's family farmers. Nelson says, "There ain't anybody in Washington I care to talk to right now," and he tells farmers that the time has come for them to act on their own behalf. He's leading by example, traveling around the country promoting local farmers' markets, organic food, and the use of biodiesel. Now there's a bandwagon I could get on.

The Turning Points

FIVE

Who Owns Rice?

The collection in the International Rice Germplasm Center is not the Institute's sole property: it belongs to the world. International cooperation in collecting, preserving, and using plant genetic resources without limitations must continue. Controversies that involve intellectual property rights and political systems need to be resolved.

KLAUS LAMPE, *director general, International Rice Research Institute (IRRI), 1991*

Mekong Delta, Vietnam

The drive from Saigon to Can Tho, a sprawling concrete city in the heart of the swampy Mekong Delta, used to take six bone-jarring hours of bumpy, horn-honking, heart-stopping, swerving, reckless driving in the searing heat. That does not include time spent waiting in sweltering traffic behind an assortment of fume-spewing vehicles to take two ferry rides across wide muddy tributaries of the Mekong River. That's what it was like in the early 1990s. Since then the road has been improved and part of the river has been bridged. What hasn't changed is the ceaseless rising and falling of the waters, the planting and harvesting of rice, and the daily rituals of the 20 million people who live here.

During rice harvest, Vietnam's roads are paved in gold. Two or three times a year, the nation's wealth is put out to dry on every available flat surface. Paddy rice, fresh from the field, is too wet to mill, so it's spread down driveways in front of palm-thatched houses and covers concrete slabs in front of shops where the men sit in plastic chairs drinking beer and ignoring deafeningly loud music. Every morning, women in conical hats pour grain out of sacks onto the roads and rake it, exposing it to the heat of the sun. If rain comes along, they rush out to cover it or quickly sweep it back into the bags. Rushing past, and somehow managing to miss the rice and each other, are rattletrap trucks, motorbikes carrying entire families, shiny black BMWs, cyclos, and pedestrians, and an occasional water buffalo plods along, led by a child holding a rope tied to its flat crescent-moon horns.

Wetland rice farming began here in the silted river basins of Asia over 7,000 years ago. There are thousands of varieties of rice known as *Oryza sativa*. The best-known are the long slender grains of *O. sativa indica* and the short oval grains of *O. sativa japonica*. Rice is so closely associated with Asian culture that its popularity in the Middle East and its African heritage are often overlooked. Rice has been grown in Africa for at least 5,000 years, particularly the *O. glaberrima* variety. The first rice grown in America came from Africa, along with slaves who were brought over specifically for their knowledge of rice and their rice-growing skills. Rice grows under a wide range of conditions and temperatures, from deep water to dry mountain slopes, and wherever it's grown, it reshapes the land. It is a generous grass, providing food for half the people on earth.

Farming in Vietnam is a combination of industrial monocropping and traditional polycultural practices, but rice is still its soul. In the past, rice was tended by hand. Portable threshers moved from field to field. Farmers took their harvest to a local miller, often by boat. Small wooden buildings scattered throughout the villages provided farmers with a place to take their paddy rice to be milled. After the "American war," foreign aid poured into the country and industrialized rice production. Roads and bridges were built to move rice around, and large rice mills that use laser-beam sorters and new rice-processing technology were constructed, returning Vietnam to its former glory as one of the world's top exporters of rice. Given the importance of rice to Vietnam, it's not surprising that during the war there, American efforts to win over the hearts and minds of the Vietnamese involved rice.

My husband and I were the first Americans to return to live in the Mekong Delta in 1994, soon after the country reopened relations with the United States. We lived in Tra Noc, just outside Can Tho, on a large government-owned rice facility my husband was helping to modernize, next to the Song Hau branch of the Mekong River. It was a collection of mills, some built during the war, some afterward, and one that had been there since the days of French occupation.

Across the road was an old airport the U.S. military had used. It was here that a young army adviser by the name of Thomas R. Hargrove landed in 1969. He was on his way to work as an agricultural specialist in Chuong Thien, an area almost completely controlled by the Vietcong, in the far south of the delta. In his memoir, *A Dragon Lives Forever,* Hargrove said, "Rice was the lifeblood of the Mekong Delta and, in a sense, what the war was all about."

Hargrove's job was to gain the trust of the area's rice farmers, then over 70 percent of the population of the delta. In 1969 there were 550,000 U.S. troops in Vietnam, and discontent with the war was rising at home. Americans wanted to begin pulling out, and part of the exit strategy was the "Vietnamization" of the war. One thing was clear to everyone: whoever was going to prevail in this sorry struggle would have to have Vietnam's rice farmers behind them. The weapon that was being used was a revolutionary new strain of rice called IR8. The "IR" came from the International Rice Research Institute (IRRI), located in the Philippines. This rice was fast to mature, short in stature, and capable of converting strong chemical fertilizers into heavy yields. And it was about to change agriculture in Asia, and history.

By the time Hargrove arrived, this new rice was being tested in small plots in the delta. He said he could "spot the semi-dwarf variety easily from choppers" because the crop "looked like it had a crew cut." While traditional taller varieties were prone to fall over, IR8 had short stems that could hold up heavy heads of grain. Hargrove says a friend of his, a researcher at IRRI and a specialist with the U.S. Agency for International Development (USAID), had smuggled IR8 seeds into Vietnam in 1967. Rumor has it that he got the seeds from someone who stole them from experimental plots at IRRI. Throughout history, valuable seeds have always been the objects of theft and intrigue, and this new rice was especially prized. Hargrove's job was to get it into the hands of farmers in the south. Previously, rice yields in the delta had averaged 1 or 1.5 metric tons per hectare (about 2.5 acres). Suddenly farmers were getting 5 or 6 tons per hectare. No wonder IR8 was called "miracle rice." In Vietnam it was *lua than nong,* or "rice of the farming god," but most farmers called it *lua Honda,* or Honda rice, because if you grew it, you could afford to buy a Honda motorcycle.

The story of the role that IR8 rice played in the war is not well known. Hargrove says he learned that the Vietcong put out orders that he was not to be killed, in order to ensure that the new seed was widely distributed in the rich wetlands of the delta. That way the Vietcong were able to get seed for themselves and smuggle it to farmers in the north. Meanwhile U.S. forces were under the impression that they had exclusive access to IRRI rice. When President Johnson visited IRRI in October 1966, he went into the fields to see IR8 firsthand. He understood its importance and made it clear at the time that his plan for peace in the region included ensuring its food security.

As an international seed bank, IRRI is committed to world food security. It's not supposed to be politically aligned. However, at that time it was staffed and funded by U.S.-aligned institutions and foundations. The Rockefeller Foundation in particular was behind the founding of the first major international seed banks and research centers, which developed what came to be known as the "green revolution" crops. These grains were remarkably productive, but their success was due as much to the vast amounts of oil-based fertilizers, pesticides, and water they used as to the skill of the institutions that bred them.

By 1968, IR8 rice was worth $1 billion. Then suddenly it became susceptible to disease and lost its economic value. IRRI quickly came up with other "improved" varieties, numbering up to IR20. When improved seeds become popular, they are often planted widely and uniformly, making them vulnerable to disease. As each one was wiped out, breeders at IRRI struggled to stay ahead of the pests. IR36 proved a more lasting success, doubling yields in some cases; it is still going strong.

IRRI's collection contains 100,000 domesticated and wild rice varieties. What that means is that for almost every blight, bug, or problem that can afflict rice, there is likely to be a variety on hand that has found a way to deal with it. The genetic resources housed at IRRI are extraordinarily valuable, and as such they are now extremely vulnerable to both corporate and government predation. When the next rice pest or blight hits, plant breeders will look to IRRI for the genes they need.

Access to these collections is a delicate diplomatic problem. The rice genome, for instance, contains thousands of genes common to *O. sativa*. And yet the governments of China and Japan, corporations like Bayer and Syngenta, and other institutions own patents on rice, various rice genes, and rice varieties. Exactly what do they own? No one really knows. While the paperwork behind a patent generally describes an ownership interest in the genetically modified molecules alone, and patent holders claim that that is their only interest, the reality of a patent, as we have seen, is that enforcement is nine tenths of the law. Since enforcement actions on patents are taken against the entire plant—for instance, when a farmer plants it without paying royalties—the existence of a patent effectively constitutes an assertion of ownership over the entire plant. We may be headed for a showdown over the ownership of rice and other valuable genetic resources, as both corporate and government patents vie for the same genes.

Where Have All the Flowers Gone?

The FAO estimates that over time, about 10,000 different plants have been used by humans for food. Of all the crops we have ever used for food, more than 75 percent are now gone. Most were lost in the past one hundred years. The causes include industrial farming practices, development, environmental degradation, modern methods of plant breeding (from hybridization to genetic engineering), and the imposition of monopoly rights that take seeds out of circulation. And intentional strategies aimed at seed varieties contribute to their loss. The Spanish organization Genetic Resources Action International (GRAIN) says that a new worldwide offensive is being launched by the global seed industry to end the practice of farm-saved seed entirely.

It used to be a given that farmers could assume they had a right to save seed. Dispersed seed saving by farmers ensured the world's food security by distributing germplasm into the hands of millions. (Germplasm is the correct technical, and more inclusive, term for seed. It refers to all plant reproductive material, including that of plants that do not reproduce by seed.) Local plant reproduction gives plants a chance to adapt to specific conditions and increases genetic diversity, something germplasm cannot do in a seed bank. Now, under international conventions, the right to save seed is an optional exception, one that requires nations to take affirmative action to put into law. The Greeks had it right when they said that Hermes was the god not just of commerce but of invention and theft as well.

Currently, according to GRAIN, two thirds of the world's crops are planted with farmer-saved seed every year. In the developing world, 80 to 90 percent of all seed used by farmers is saved seed. In the rest of the world it's between 30 and 60 percent. Seed saving is invariably a culturally bound practice that ties communities together economically and ecologically. The practice of seed saving ensures the health and resiliency of the world's food and medicinal plants. But it's not just third world farmers who are affected; seed ownership affects us all.

Take, for instance, that popular feeding trough the salad bar. In the 1980s we began filling our plates with mixed lettuce, cherry tomatoes, cucumbers, baby spinach, and blanched broccoli, all colorfully arrayed under a glass "sneeze shield." Grocery stores and fast-food chains soon began carrying ready-to-eat salads, and the vegetable seed industry, which until the 1990s had been the neglected stepsister of the biotechnology boom, began attracting the attention of the bioengineers. Previously, all their investment had gone into commodity crops like corn, soy, and cotton. They weren't even looking at lettuce.

One man did see the potential in the $80 billion North American fresh produce market: Mexican billionaire Alfonso Romo Garza. He got busy gobbling up vegetable seed companies, and by 1999 his company, Seminis Seeds, controlled 40 percent of vegetables sold in the United States. According to the *Wall Street Journal,* his revenue from seed was twice that of his closest rival, Novartis. Romo became known as the "king of vegetables," but he wanted more; he wanted to play god. Already his gift to the world was a low-heat jalapeño pepper and those ubiquitous two-inch orange bullets we call baby carrots. He had plans to create nonbrowning lettuce and tearless onions. But all too soon, Romo's fortunes began to wilt.

By the year 2000, Seminis had become the world's largest vegetable seed company, listing 8,000 varieties of 60 different species of fruits and vegetables. It had 70 research stations, seed production sites in 32 countries, and sales in 120 countries. Romo was unfazed by consumer rejection of transgenic vegetables, saying that he would change our eating habits. Sounding very much like the Bill Gates of produce, he said that he had the money and he had the seeds, adding that "seeds are software." He boasted that 80 percent of fresh produce in the United States would be transgenic by 2009.

Seminis grew the same way all seed companies are growing these days, by buying up smaller companies. It bought the garden (fruit and vegetable) seed divisions of larger companies like Asgrow. Then the company went into business with Monsanto, developing Roundup Ready lettuce and tomatoes. They had transgenic squash, melons, peas, carrots, and cucumbers in the works, all using popular varieties owned by Seminis. The problem with getting into bed with Monsanto, however, as thousands of farmers and seed companies have found out, is that only one of you gets up the next morning.

Monsanto began buying up its competition in the mid-1990s. Like all the big agrochemical/pharmaceutical companies, who were repositioning themselves as "life science" companies, with a stated goal of owning and profiting from all the world's plant germplasm, Monsanto started out developing and licensing its technology. It was making about $100 per bag of seed but soon realized that it had to keep its rivals from copying that seed, so it started buying the companies it had been licensing to, and the race was on.

In 1996, Monsanto began by buying Agracetus, a subsidiary of W. R. Grace, for $150 million. Then it bought Calgene—of Flavr Savr tomato fame—for $340 million. The size and number of deals quickly accelerated. Monsanto bought Dekalb for $2.3 billion, and in 1997, Monsanto paid Holden Seeds a price that was twenty-three times its annual earnings. Why? Because it wasn't just about these companies' assets, it was about owning the parent seed lines and getting control of the genetics. Monsanto bought seed companies in India and Brazil as well as Unilever's European wheat-breeding business and Cargill's international seed operations for $1.4 billion.

Between 1996 and 1998, Monsanto spent a total of $8 billion acquiring or establishing ownership interests in U.S. and foreign seed companies. That forced Dow, Bayer, and others to try to keep up. In one move, DuPont Corporation became the world's largest seed supplier by buying Pioneer Hi-Bred International for $7.7 billion. One industry executive said in *SeedQuest,* an industry newsletter, that any seed company that thinks it can remain independent is "living in a dream world." And he predicted that as soon as these companies gained control over the market, they'd raise their prices. The end of the Seminis story is that Monsanto bought the company in 2005, overtaking DuPont as the world's largest seed company. Monsanto will strengthen its position on top when it acquires Delta & Pine Land cotton seed company.

The ETC Group has been tracking the increasing control and concentration of the seed industry. In 1997, under its former name, RAFI, the ETC said that just ten seed corporations controlled 40 percent of the world's seed market. Then, in 2005, it reported that the top ten companies controlled 50 percent of commercial seed sales. In 1996, there were ten major agrochemical companies. In 2000, only five were left. Previously, until the 1970s, seeds were distributed widely through the public sector, small seed suppliers, family farmers, and regional seed companies. Now there are only four giant agrochemical seed suppliers: Monsanto, DuPont/Pioneer Hi-Bred, Syngenta, and Dow.

Can Private Seeds Meet Public Needs?

The concentration of seed ownership has had a devastating impact on public plant-breeding programs as well. A report published by the USDA's Economic Research Service (ERS) says that because of seed industry consolidation, research and development over the past thirty years has shifted from the public to the private sector. Funding for private-sector research doubled during that time and now far exceeds public spending. Public investment in plant breeding has not increased. Biotechnology is expensive; Syngenta, for instance, spent $822 million on R&D in 2005. Those expenses and the availability of germplasm are the deciding factors in determining what studies are done, what plants are bred, and who benefits. The increasing concentration of seed ownership limits both the number and the kinds of plants available to breeders too.

The ERS found another interesting connection between consolidation and research. Using econometric methods, it discovered that instead of competing with each other to develop more and different kinds of seeds, private companies are increasingly focused on expanding their market share for fewer varieties. Just when we need plant breeding to focus on ecological adaptability, to help us cope with changing climate conditions, the private sector is focusing on a narrow range of crop varieties for their economic potential instead. The ERS also noted that when public research on corn, soy, and cotton was increased, it stimulated similar research in the private sector.

Private seed companies tend to concentrate on and preserve only those varieties that have some commercial potential. When Seminis got into economic trouble, it cut costs by reducing its seed inventory by 25 percent, and just like that, 2,000 varieties of seed were lost. Private breeding programs also contribute to the loss of genetic material, because they are concerned with the more profitable uniform varieties or those that can be bred for industrial uses, especially hybrid and patented varieties. As a result, older open-pollinated varieties are disappearing. As they vanish and specialized seeds take over, industrialization is intensified.

Seed Savers Exchange (SSE) monitors the loss of heritage seed. It says that of the 5,000 nonhybrid vegetable varieties that were available in 1981 seed catalogs, 88 percent had been dropped by 1998. During those years, one quarter of mail-order seed companies in the United States and Canada had gone out of business or been acquired. In Europe, only registered seed can be sold for garden use, and many old varieties are not registered.

In the public sector, policies and budget constraints often reduce the availability of seeds and support for public plant breeding. As of 2004, substantial numbers of European farmers—88 percent in Spain, 46 percent in Germany, and 30 percent in the UK—were still using farm-saved seed. But a single policy change can cause a major change on the ground. When Spain began linking the use of certified seed to farm subsidies during the 1990s, it led to a 75 percent increase in the use of certified seed by farmers.

In another policy move, the European Community (EC) decided to combine all the plant varieties listed by its member states into one "Common Catalogue" in 1980. The ETC Group reported that seed companies provided the EC with a "hit list" of

1,500 plant names they said were duplicates. These synonymous varieties were then eliminated, over the protests of groups who claimed that many of them were unique. One English organization said that only 38 percent of these seeds were duplicates; the rest were simply varieties that no one "owned." Eventually another 1,000 distinct but low-profit or nonproprietary varieties were eliminated from the catalog. Dutch plant breeder Jaap Hardon says that seed legislation in the EU reflects "how the law protects specific interests at the expense of well-founded biological rationale and public interest."

We are now operating agriculture on the assumption that farmers are unable to manage their own biodiversity. When farmers are no longer allowed to save and breed plants, it will mean the end of one of the most ingenious, resilient, and economically autonomous systems of production the world has ever known. Allowing the world's natural wealth of seed to be transferred to the private sector is a fundamental social error. The public and private sectors have completely different purposes and operate by different processes. There is no possible way that these two entities can be considered equivalent providers of something as important as food for the world.

This trend toward seed consolidation is linked to another, even larger overall trend toward corporate concentration in the agricultural sector. A 2001 study by the National Farmers Union found that a few clusters of linked corporations now control the production, processing, distribution, and retailing of most of the grains, meats, and dairy products we eat. Now just four multinational agrochemical corporations decide what plants are grown, what foods and drugs are produced, and what price will be paid for many of life's basic necessities. These corporations are strengthening their grip on all aspects of the food system. Genetic engineering and its patented products are both a tool for accomplishing this control and an end in themselves. Companies want market control; governments want political control. Either way, when these organizations exert top-down control over the food supply, ordinary people no longer have a say over what they eat.

Since seeds are the first link in the food chain, when they are owned by a few multinational corporations, those corporations, and not the citizens of the world, will decide the future of food. This change, from a people-centered food system to a privately controlled one, represents a monumental turning point in the way society functions, but it has been a largely silent, unnoticed transformation.

Can Biotechnology Feed the World?

There is a legitimate question to be asked about how we should go about meeting the increasing need for food and energy as world populations grow and resources shrink. The FAO estimates that about 850 million people go hungry every day and another 1 billion are living on less than one dollar. Hunger stalks people everywhere, including America. It takes a daily toll on the body and the spirit. In the third world, the raw and bitter injustice of hunger and poverty is not hidden from view. But neither are the resilient and sophisticated survival strategies of the poor.

Industry wants to make this issue about its technology. If the technology question were put fairly, it would be phrased more like, "What agricultural technologies are best in a given situation, to increase value to the farmer and maintain human and environmental health?" Asking "Can biotechnology feed the world?" is a setup. Of course it can. Industrial agriculture can too. Both technologies produce massive quantities of food. It's just that they are not the optimal approach, considering that they rely on shaky science, the accumulation of private wealth, and poor social policy.

Hunger is caused by poverty. And since poverty is a political problem, it cannot be cured by commercial technology—or any technology, for that matter. As long-time hunger expert Frances Moore Lappé reminds us, hunger is not caused by a lack of food. There's more than enough food in the world to feed everyone today. Famine is a function of how food is distributed, and that is always a political issue. During the time of "the great hunger" in Ireland in the mid-nineteenth century, Britain was exporting food, giving rise to the expression that "God may have created the potato blight, but the British caused the famine."

Lappé says that the question of whether or not GMOs will feed the world is simply a way for "self-interested corporations to reinforce the myth that our planet's problem is scarcity, from which only their products can save us." The real problem, she says, is actually the overproduction that these corporations and their friends in government create. Blame can also be laid at the doorstep of our trade and aid policies, which are forcing the poor to buy food instead of being able to grow it themselves.

Speaking from the point of view of the third world, Nobel Peace Prize laureate Wangari Maathai has been an outspoken critic of agricultural biotechnology. She says, "The idea that African farmers should have to buy seeds, developed from their own biological materials, from transnational corporations, because such companies have given themselves the exclusive rights to those seeds, is outrageous... If we thought that slavery and colonialism were gross violations of human rights, we have to wake up to what is awaiting us down the secretive road of biopiracy, patenting of life and genetic engineering. Genocide from hunger, such as we have not yet seen, becomes a haunting possibility."

The story that best illustrates Maathai's point and best underscores the fact that biotechnology is not the way to feed the world is the story of golden rice. For years the agricultural biotechnology industry worked behind the scenes and spent millions of dollars searching for something that would make it look good. It found it in golden rice. Rice is a natural choice, since most of the world's poor depend on it for their main sustenance, and in many places rice is synonymous with food. In Vietnam, the word for "food" is the same as the word for "rice."

So with great fanfare, in 1999, the industry announced that its researchers had created something that would benefit the needy. They'd engineered rice laced with beta carotene, which the body converts into an essential nutrient, vitamin A. This was said to be a cure for vitamin A deficiency (VAD), which causes blindness and weakened immune systems in millions of poor people and can lead to death from disease. Daffodil genes were used to provide the beta carotene. They gave the rice a yellow color; hence its name.

The press picked up on this development, and it was lauded as a great technological achievement. It was a "taste of things to come," according to colorful full-page ads placed in major newspapers by the industry under the name the Council for Biotechnology Information. The cover of *Time* magazine, playing the biotechnology industry's tune about how they were the good guys and the critics were the problem, said, "This rice could save a million kids a year…but protestors believe such genetically modified foods are bad for us and our planet."

In *Safe Food,* nutritionist Marion Nestle traces the complex technical steps it took to produce rice that would provide vitamin A. First, she says, consider that the Rockefeller Foundation spends $4 million a year on genetically engineering rice and that it was a major contributor to the development of golden rice. The long, involved, expensive research done to develop this new product produced two things: rice that was edible and a "thicket of intellectual property rights claims." By some counts, as many as seventy patents were taken out on various parts of its construction. Monsanto and AstraZeneca, who own the technology, say they will forgo their patents and donate the rice to IRRI and poor farmers. "These concessions appear exceedingly generous," says Nestle, except that this rice "is unlikely to have much commercial potential in developing countries. Its public relations value, however, is enormous."

Nestle is one of the most respected nutritionists in the country. After she did her reasoned analysis of golden rice, she appealed to professional organizations to weigh in as well. The response surprised her. She says she came to realize that her profession thinks that "complex social problems—in this case malnutrition—are more easily solved by private sector, commercially driven science than by societal decisions and political actions."

Their responses, she said, also implied that anyone who questioned "the potential value of golden rice bears moral responsibility for 500,000 cases of childhood blindness."

Others saw the early praise for golden rice as premature and decided to do their own testing before making public pronouncements. Greenpeace, for instance, found that there was so little beta carotene in golden rice that for adults to get the vitamin benefit, they would have to eat twenty pounds of it every day. Greenpeace said it was shameful that industry would promote this sham as a solution to VAD, calling it a "fool's gold" intended to bolster the health of the industry, not the poor. But the industry says that environmental and consumer organizations that oppose its products are standing in the way of using genetic technologies to benefit the poor. The activists respond by saying that the industry is advancing the cause of biotechnology by using "moral blackmail."

In 2001, Bill Freese, a policy analyst at Friends of the Earth, studied the risks and benefits of golden rice and the problem of vitamin A deficiency. He also looked at the rice itself and pointed out that children, the ones most in need, would have to eat twelve pounds of the rice daily to get the intended benefit. He added that such a lopsided diet would lack many other nutrients the body needs. Plus, anyone suffering from diarrhea, the most common ailment in the developing world, would not derive any vitamin A from the golden rice.

The malnutrition associated with rice and the diet of the poor is caused by multiple factors that cannot be fixed by one GMO, even if it did work as intended. John R. Lupien, the director of the Food and Nutrition Division of the FAO, says that "a single-nutrient approach towards a nutrition-related public health problem is usually, with the exception of perhaps iodine or selenium deficiencies, neither feasible nor desirable."

What most people don't know is that beta carotene is present in rice bran but is destroyed when rice is milled. The reason rice is milled to the point where it is white is that in the places where white rice is the staple—the tropics and the undeveloped world—

it stores well. The bran in brown rice spoils quickly. If people don't add greens or other sources of vitamins to their diet, they can suffer from VAD. Solving a terrible problem like VAD is a laudable goal, but using GMOs to alter a beloved food like rice would impose unacceptable cultural changes on the intended beneficiaries. The color of rice is an important attribute. And which would you prefer, one twenty-pound bowl of a grain with everything you need engineered into it or a mixture of naturally produced grains, greens, fish, and fruit? Taking the proponents of golden rice at face value, they seem to be asking the poor to eat one giant bowl of transgenic rice while they themselves would only consider eating a varied diet.

The biotechnology industry, which is made up of pharmaceutical and agrochemical companies that regularly flood the third world with poisonous chemicals, has repeatedly shown itself to be incapable of respecting the basic dignity of the poor and to act responsibly in matters of public health. Its chemical and genetic technologies are not more productive than appropriate technologies, so why should we even consider giving these companies responsibility for feeding the world? India's leading environmentalist, Vandana Shiva, says that GMO rice is "part of a package of globalized agriculture which is actually creating malnutrition." Her concern is that these commercial technological solutions will create new food-safety risks, introduce novel substances that pose new health risks into the diet of the poor, and still do nothing to help the poor with their nutrition. Shiva says that the women farmers she works with in Bengal use more than a hundred plants as leafy green vegetables, a rich source of vitamin A.

Some early supporters of vitamin A rice and biotechnology have had to concede that they missed the mark. Gordon Conway, president of the Rockefeller Foundation at the time, said that "the public relations uses of golden rice have gone too far. The industry's advertisements and the media in general seem to forget that it is a research product that needs considerable further development before it will be available to farmers and consumers." Really? Those advertisements were designed to make people think this rice was being eaten and saving lives today.

What's important about this issue is not who's right or wrong. What's important is how to solve hunger and poverty-related suffering. If golden rice is the best that all the wealth and expertise the biotechnology industry can bring to this issue, it doesn't bode well for the industry's case for being the protector of the poor. As Dr. Richard Horton, editor of the British science journal *The Lancet*, says, "Seeking a technological food fix for world hunger may be ... the most commercially malevolent wild goose chase of the new century."

Bill Freese says that not only would golden rice create more problems than it solves, it's simply not the best use of limited public funds. Why not help the poor grow vitamin-rich vegetables such as beans and pumpkins, as a project in Bangladesh is doing, or copy nutrition education programs that use radio and street theater to remind people to combine their foods, as some Asian countries do? Others are raising nutrition levels simply by growing fish in the rice paddies that people can use to supplement their diet.

Small-scale projects like this are more effective at increasing the capacity of the poor to address their problems and to feed themselves. But, says Hans Herren, winner of the 1995 World Food Prize, these projects don't get funded because half of the Rockefeller Foundation's budget for agriculture is going to fund its interests in biotechnology. And now that the Gates Foundation and other high-technology-oriented sources of money are getting involved in hunger issues, the inexpensive, low-technology, locally based solutions will not be getting the support they need. Who, then, should bear responsibility for all this preventable suffering? A report by Christian Aid, "Biotechnology and GMOs," says that "biotechnology and GM crops are taking us down a dangerous road, creating the classic conditions for hunger, poverty and even famine. Ownership and control concentrated in too few hands and a food supply based on too few varieties planted widely are the worst option for food security."

Who Really Feeds the World?

I learned a great deal while I was living in Vietnam. My husband and I did what we could to help those in need and to learn from the land and the people there. I had an organic farm near the Mekong River. Since I couldn't find vegetables that were not doused with chemicals, I decided to grow my own. I hired a farmer and his water buffalo to till up a few acres and then spent almost a year figuring out how to transplant the skills I had honed in a California garden to a tropical swamp in the Mekong Delta. Soon things were growing, and I turned the project into a demonstration farm. I noticed that many women took home chemicals from the rice fields and were using them indiscriminately in their household gardens. So, after learning how to grow local plants organically, I invited women from a nearby village in and served them lunch. Then I took them around the farm and showed them how they could grow their gardens without toxic chemicals.

There is a reason that I chose to focus on women. As I traveled around the country, I was fascinated by the hand labor used to farm, especially rice. In California, there's not a soul to be seen in the rice fields, where the crop is planted and sprayed by airplane and harvested by machine. In Vietnam, much of the work is still done by hand. In the newly planted rice paddies, for instance, it's common to see long lines of eight or ten people bent over from the waist, their hands in the mud, transplanting rice seedlings. Whenever I stopped to listen to their chatter or singing or just to watch how they worked, they would stand up and wave. Invariably, this chorus line of fieldworkers was almost all women. It turns out that women do much of the work of transplanting, weeding, and harvesting rice.

The FAO estimates that in parts of Asia and Africa, women do 85 percent or more of agricultural fieldwork. Women are the key to food production everywhere. They work on the farm, they tend their own gardens, and they do the marketing and cooking. And yet the particular needs and contributions of women are seldom taken into consideration when agricultural development decisions are made. Aid consultants who advise third world governments favor projects that provide paid jobs for men, those that use machinery, and those that move the economy toward the industrial model.

Giving women education and even tiny amounts of economic power, along with the trust and encouragement of their communities, is essential to economic development. The work of the 2006 Nobel Peace Prize winner Muhammad Yunus and the microlending strategy have clearly demonstrated that point. And while everyone in Vietnam was very hardworking, women were performing incredible feats of physical labor, often for little or no pay. Their contributions have often been neglected when government agencies make decisions about how to allocate resources.

I will always remember one woman I saw regularly in Vietnam. She worked at the rice mill as a laborer, the lowest rung of the unskilled labor force, the working poor. In the evenings after the mills shut down, she would show up now and then, and I would watch the way she'd forage for food. She would harvest water hyacinths along the river or pull green papayas from trees living at the edge of the jungle. One late afternoon I saw her sitting on the ground near a huge pile of rice hulls. All I could see was her polyester blouse sticking to her rounded back, wet with perspiration from the heat, and the back of her hat. She would lean forward, pick up a handful of hulls, and then let them fall through her fingers. Every once in a while she would catch a single grain of rice and carefully put in it a bamboo tray at her side. She sat and sifted for hours. Eventually, when she had gleaned a cup or two of rice, she left. I never knew her name or how many people depended on her for food, but I will always remember her quiet dignity and monumental patience. To me, she demonstrated an essential truth about how the world gets fed. The work of feeding the world is done by the hands of women.

SIX

The Botany of Scarcity

The crops that feed the world are on a collision
course with climate change, water, energy constraints and expanding populations. A perfect
storm is brewing.

CARY FOWLER,
Global Crop Diversity Trust

Svalbard, Norway

Teams of scientists from all over the globe have gathered here to
measure the glaciers, check changes in air temperature and sea
levels, and calculate the rising amount of CO_2 in the atmosphere.
They are working out models and predictions for how much
time the world as we know it has left. Meanwhile, outside the
human settlements, reindeer roaming on the tundra are getting
tangled in discarded measuring instruments, and polar bears are
shuffling around looking for food, having been forced ashore by
melting ice.

"Svalbard is a place to watch like a hawk," says journalist Fred
Pearce, because of its sensitivity to changing climate conditions
and because of the sheer amount of scientific study that goes
on here. And, I would add, because this is where the Doomsday
Vault is under construction. Plans call for drilling a tunnel deep
into the mountainside, ending in two large rooms. Once completed, these rooms will have the capacity to store 3 million seeds,

samples that will be taken from every agriculturally useful plant in the world and kept for as long as they might be needed. The Doomsday Vault is the world's newest and most innovative seed bank, but it's based on the very old idea that we should save seeds in times of calamity. It's a Noah's Ark for agriculture. As it is being constructed, the air is warming, the ice is melting, the wildlife is getting restless, and the humans are running around, some measuring everything in sight and others storing up supplies for the coming changes in the weather. Svalbard is quickly becoming the stage set for the unfolding drama of our current environmental crisis.

Cary Fowler, director of the Global Crop Diversity Trust, is the person responsible for gathering the seeds as well as the public and financial support needed for this undertaking. Fowler has a great deal of credibility in both international circles and the nongovernmental community. He has been an outspoken critic of the impact that industrial agriculture has been having on plant diversity. In 1990, he wrote the seminal work on the topic, *Shattering,* with Pat Mooney, who is now with the ETC Group. Fowler is a tall, thin, amiable American, with traces of his southern origins still in his voice. He makes his case for the work of the trust in carefully reasoned and emotionally compelling language.

Fowler says that press reports about how the vault is intended to serve humanity in the event of a global catastrophe tell only half the story. The vault will also function as a backup storage system for the world's seed banks, and they will have access to the material if it is needed. The samples that seed banks contribute to the vault will be labeled and categorized by the banks themselves; the trust will not touch what's put in storage. The trust's other projects are devoted to supporting seed banks, providing them with secure funding, and helping them inventory and describe their existing collections.

Seed banks face three main challenges, says Fowler: a lack of secure funding, issues of management and expertise, and vulnerability to natural disasters. He points to the damage that was done to a seed bank in Southeast Asia by a recent typhoon, which caused the loss of rare seeds. Sometimes financial constraints mean that material just sits and deteriorates or is not replenished on time. When seed banks fail to maintain their collections, those varieties are lost forever. It makes sense to invest in a secure backup system that would protect the 6 million seed samples now being stored in seed banks throughout the world. This is not your ordinary backup system, however. Fowler says the vault will be the "most secure conservation facility in the world by several orders of magnitude."

The trust is governed by a board that is appointed by international groups, mainly those involved in the International Treaty on Plant Genetics, as well as the United Nations and the Consultative Group on International Agricultural Research (CGIAR). So far it appears to be operating in a fairly transparent manner, posting information about its donors and governing mechanisms on its website. Most of the funding for the trust comes from institutions like the World Bank, CGIAR, participating countries, a few very large foundations, and some corporations. DuPont/Pioneer Hi-Bred and Syngenta each gave it $1 million, and $5 million came from Australian grain growers. The Bill and Melinda Gates Foundation gave the trust $30 million, and Norway contributed another $7.5 million to fund a separate crop-diversity preservation initiative.

When the suggestion that whoever pays the piper calls the tune comes up, Fowler bristles. He says that anyone who suggests this collection could in any way fall prey to private interests is misinformed, and he challenges them to demonstrate how that might happen. For now, it appears to be a situation in which the corporate donors are afforded an opportunity to do a bit of green washing. DuPont/Pioneer's announcement of its gift mentions that the collections are public and freely available to all under the treaty. It pays homage to the need for diversity and says the company hopes its contribution will "spark dialogue about the importance of preserving genetic resources [and] bring greater value to farmers and improved products to consumers." DuPont's press release refers to its work to "protect crop genetic resources to promote sustainable agriculture." But DuPont's environmental record of chemical pollution and Pioneer's indiscriminate use of GMOs in the field make any claims that they care about sustainable agriculture sound hypocritical.

The problem with taking funding from corporations whose policies you oppose is that the giving may reflect well on the donor but the organization can be tainted by the gift. The source of funding for this effort is not by any means the most important issue. As seed-saving efforts go, the Crop Trust is the best there is. The question is, why is the Doomsday Vault even needed? To answer that, we need to understand the role of seed banks and their methods of seed saving and redistribution. Many seed banks like to quote the late Jack Harlan, who said, "These resources stand between us and catastrophic starvation on a scale we cannot imagine. In a very real sense, the future of the human race rides on these materials." But are they the real keepers of the treasure, or do the farmers and planters still hold the keys?

"The Original Monies of the Earth"

All the material needed to propagate the world's most important agricultural plants has already been collected and is being stored in large and small seed banks scattered all over the world. Some of these seeds are poorly stored in paper bags and jars put on dusty shelves, and some of them are vacuum-packed in foil bags and carefully arranged in state-of-the-art freezers. There are small, local, independent seed collections that serve farmers and traditional breeders, but in general the seeds that are stored in the big seed banks are not local seeds. Most seed banks store material that came from elsewhere, particularly the third world. The traditional farmers who developed our main agricultural crop plants have been engaged in what sociologist Jack Kloppenburg calls "a massive program of foreign aid." They have donated their seeds, by choice or by expropriation, to governments, quasi-public seed banks, and corporations, which then transform them into their own highly valued property but do not share the benefits gained from these seeds with the people whose skill and knowledge originally developed them.

There are about 1,400 seed banks in the world. And although there has been an explosion in the number of seed banks, they aren't necessarily saving any more kinds of seeds. What they're saving is mostly duplicates of each other's seeds. In the 1970s there was only a handful of long-term seed-saving facilities in the world. Then collectors went on a worldwide binge, and by 1985 gene banks in 72 countries were holding 2.5 million accessions, or separate samples. By 1996, collections in 137 countries were holding 6.2 million accessions. Fowler calls this "gene inflation," and he says it's a real headache, because seed banks are just "trading samples back and forth with each other in a totally uncoordinated and basically unknown way" and creating a lot of "unintended duplication." There are actually only about 2 million unique seed samples in seed banks, but the rest are millions and millions of accessions.

Each collection is like a snapshot of the plants collected at any one time. It cannot possibly represent all possible variations of a plant variety, so what is selected immediately narrows the amount of germplasm that gets saved. Many collections store only what was gathered in the last forty or fifty years and thus are limited to what was collectible during that time. That's how the collections are formed. The other half of the story is what happens to a seed once it is deposited in a seed bank. Each sample —a seed, a leaf, or a stem—also has to survive the process of collection, repeated handling, transporting, and storage. These are all living things, so they are easily damaged and they age and die. All material kept in seed banks has to be constantly regrown, its life renewed. All collections regenerate their germplasm according to their own standards.

Serious problems can arise when a bank's samples are regenerated, which is usually done in the open air. At that time the plants are vulnerable to contamination, from any pathogens in the area, from cross-pollination, and from exposure to GMOs. Available growing areas are extremely limited, as are budgets.

Sometimes even the most obvious precautions are ignored. In the case of the world's largest collection of peas, which is housed in a gene bank in Germany, the Munich Environmental Institute reported in 2007 that several hundred samples were being grown out in an open field, only 500 meters from a field that was being used to test transgenic potatoes containing a cholera bacterium and a rabbit virus. These crops ordinarily would not mix, but why take chances, given how little we really know about gene flow?

There have been unconfirmed reports that some CGIAR collections are contaminated with GMOs. The curators deny it, but it may be only a matter of time. The ETC Group watches CGIAR carefully and reports that it has been "huddling with the biotech industry" to craft a policy response to GMO contamination, which the industry refers to as "adventitious presence," as if it were unavoidable.

Inside, seed banks aren't very complicated. They all basically use cold storage in one form or another. The Doomsday Vault is just one very big freezer. The complexity enters in when it comes to cataloging the collection and devising information systems that provide access and research data. Two of the most important functions of a seed bank are to describe what's in the collection and to figure out how to retrieve that material and make it useful. The human element comes in when managers and plant experts make decisions about what gets preserved and why. This is where ex-situ seed banks ("ex situ" is the term used for seed banks and collections where reproductive plant material is kept in storage, out of its natural context) cross the line from being conservation-oriented to becoming economic institutions. They are called banks, after all.

Not everyone thinks that ex-situ collections are the best way to save plant germplasm. Many botanists, farmers, and environmentalists want to see plants preserved where they grow, and they want more attention and support for in-situ seed saving, where plants are preserved in their natural habitat or on farms and in gardens. Some nongovernmental organizations, particularly those that are working to protect the rights of small farmers and that want to keep plant breeding public, are critical of ex-situ seed banks. They're concerned about the impact that international trade, intellectual property rights, and international aid strategies are having on local seed saving.

In-situ strategies save plants in the places where they grow best. These efforts can conserve more diversity than gene banks for several reasons. Gene banks tend to focus only on what can be stored. Living collections can grow more kinds of plants as well as their wild and weedy relatives. Local seed saving can tap into local knowledge of little-known and rare varieties. These place-based collections are better tuned into the needs of traditional farmers and tend to specialize in culturally significant plants. Some plant breeders have suggested that in-situ collections do not make their germplasm available to breeders and it's difficult to find out what they have in their collections. Others point out that these collections are more vulnerable to environmental and political changes than seed banks and that just because they are in situ does not mean they're free of government or corporate predation.

The difference is that for in-situ collections, the seeds themselves are the primary value. In seed banks, more value is placed on the usefulness and retrievability of what is in the collection. Seed banking is expensive and not necessarily reliable, so very few seed banks can afford to concentrate on saving what exists for its own sake. Saving something that needs to be saved, or just because it is threatened, is rare. Few major seed banks still take in much wild seed. The one world-class seed bank that saves wild seed is the UK's Millennium Seed Bank, which just added its billionth seed, an African bamboo from Mali.

Critics of the Doomsday Vault say that all the millions being spent on it and all the money directed at ex-situ seed banking should be directed toward preserving in-situ collections and that more funding should go toward protecting seed saving by traditional farmers. In the long run, in-situ strategies are the most cost-effective way to save diversity. For thousands of years—in fact, right up to the mid-twentieth century—seeds didn't need to be "saved" by institutions. The rise of seed banks has occurred at the same time that the role of the farmer has been compromised and corporations have taken over plant breeding. The concentration of ownership of seeds in private hands is part of the reason in-situ seed saving is in trouble.

The choice of which strategy to support, in situ or ex situ, turns on whether you want to support the economic or the ecological values of seeds. Deciding between the two often depends on whether you see the world as a marketplace or as a community. Fortunately, we really don't have to choose. The world can afford to do both, at least in theory. The problem arises in the choosing. In practice, big seed banks siphon funding, expertise, and public attention away from other, equally important seed conservation strategies. They often claim the moral high ground and operate in ways that discourage farm seed saving. When they position themselves in such a way as to say that they, and not farmers, are the "best" seed savers, then they are forcing funders to choose them over the farmers. This is the mentality of scarcity, and it is a false choice, as all scarcity strategies are. Both methods of preservation can be useful. However, both need to reemphasize the public interest. The rise of seed banking and the demise of the small farmer have turned agricultural seed saving on its head. The solution lies in putting the farmer, instead of agribusiness, back on top as the primary actor and beneficiary of all seed-saving strategies.

Green Revolution or Gene Revolution?

The biggest player in international seed banking is CGIAR. It operates sixteen international independent plant research centers, a dozen of which have their own gene banks. Taken together, CGIAR centers hold the world's largest collections of seed. A brief look at the list of CGIAR centers provides a glimpse into the enormous complexity involved in working with one hundred different participating countries. There are two tropical agriculture centers, one in Africa and one in Colombia; another for the semiarid tropics in India; one for livestock in Africa; a forest center in Indonesia; a corn and wheat center in Mexico; a potato headquarters in Peru; a center for research in "dry areas" in Syria; several places for tree diversity and fish research; policy research centers in Europe and Washington, D.C.; and rice centers in the Philippines and West Africa.

The principal purpose of most seed banks is to preserve their germplasm for all humanity. Their mission statements, and some of their work, often reflect this value. But it does not always work as intended. The way seed banks are funded and managed and the way they make their collections accessible to breeders have produced an incoherent system that does not function in the best interests of the public.

Nazreen Kadir, a scientist who was raised in South America and is now a mother and community activist in northern California, wrote her Ph.D. dissertation in 2004 on ownership, use, and access issues in "public trust crop germplasm," particularly in the CGIAR centers. Kadir says that the world's gene banks are not rising to the challenge of preserving the world's seed heritage for the good of all. They are in danger of becoming "publicly funded repositories for private interests," she says. She points to the role Novartis/Syngenta has played in governing the work of the International Maize and Wheat Improvement Center, known by its Spanish acronym, CIMMYT, the world's largest collection of wheat and corn seed, located in Mexico. Kadir lived at the CIMMYT facility while doing her research and used it as a case study for her overall assessment of the CGIAR centers. She cites documented evidence that an "anti-hunger and pro-poor proposal" which favored farmers was turned down for funding in favor of a biotechnology-based proposal by the Novartis Foundation, which has a place on CIMMYT's board.

These powerful international centers of plant breeding know they play a crucial role in ensuring the world's food security, and yet they are increasingly partnering with corporations. Officially, the CGIAR system has called for a halt to the patenting of germplasm coming from its collections. It is also working to end abuses of the system used for seed exchange, which relies on trust and which has put public-domain germplasm in the hands of private companies. In 1998, two Australian research institutes claimed patent rights over chickpea seeds that came from CGIAR's Semi-Arid Tropics Institute in India. That matter was quickly resolved, but seed bank watchers say the threat remains.

GRAIN says that Mexican farmers provided 91 percent of the corn germplasm being stored at CIMMYT and that over 93 percent of the rice collection at IRRI came from farmers in developing countries such as Indonesia, Bangladesh, India, and China. CGIAR shares its collections with national research scientists and financial donors in the north, without compensation to the south. GRAIN says that CGIAR "claims credit" for distributing the benefits of its collection back to farmers and developing countries, often in the form of "improved" varieties, but it does not take into account that its new varieties often cost more, are more expensive to grow, and are replacing local varieties.

What bothers Pat Mooney, who continues to monitor CGIAR, is that the real stakeholders in this issue, the farmers whose livelihoods depend on CGIAR's seed, are not being consulted. The ETC Group, along with 144 other civil society organizations, is pressuring CGIAR to come to terms with these issues. Overall, Mooney says, some promising projects have come from the CGIAR system, but he says he's been "deeply unimpressed." While great people have been involved in these efforts, he suggests that the $400 million these organizations spend might be put to better uses. These critiques of CGIAR have been simmering for over fifteen years, and to its credit, CGIAR acknowledges them. That said, whoever has the key or access codes to these vaults can use them however they want—as a treasure chest, a war chest, or a medicine chest.

After years of contention over who has access to public and nongovernmental seed resources, some progress toward an international agreement was made and a new international legal framework governing seeds was adopted in 2001. It's called the International Treaty on Plant Genetic Resources for Food and

Agriculture. The treaty recognizes the right of each nation to its own seed collections. It has been signed by seventy-seven countries and the European Union, with the United States and Japan abstaining. It's fairly comprehensive and has been harmonized with the Convention on Biological Diversity. However, it covers only sixty-four of the most important food and forage crops.

If the treaty works as intended, it will help govern the world's seed conservation strategies with some hope for equity among nations. It provides for a multilateral system of access to germplasm by plant breeders and for benefit sharing from the commercial use of these resources. It could provide an opportunity for world governments to act responsibly and make sure plant genetic resources are properly conserved, available to all, and remain in the public domain. The treaty holds that intellectual property rights must not be claimed for any germplasm obtained from its participants, but the mechanisms for enforcing this principle are unclear. In 2006 several other important issues were still being worked out.

Many seed banks do work for the benefit of humanity and they are staffed by dedicated people. But even the best seed banks, if badly managed, can easily become seed morgues. Their fortunes often rise and fall along with those of the countries that host them. But money was not what most worried the seed bank experts I talked to. What concerned them was the rapid loss of expertise in seed conservation and plant breeding. There always used to be a group of people who were willing to devote their lives to a particular plant and who knew it in all its permutations. When pests or crop failures hit, they knew which variety might solve the problem, and they could be counted on to find the answers.

Plant breeders all have their favorite stories about some rare plant that saved the day and how some old guy sitting in a dusty storeroom knew just where it was being kept or where it was growing in the field. What all these stories turn on is the fact that when it comes to finding a solution to the threats to plants, there's no substitute for human experience and expertise. The essential link in seed preservation has always been in the relationship between the seed and the human being, but that is being lost. Biology has become a largely computational endeavor. Inventories are computerized and seed characteristics are being reduced to what we know of their genetic traits. Now, if it's not in the database, it doesn't exist.

There are plenty of reasons, then, to agree with the trust that its plan to back up the world's seed collections and strengthen the current seed banking system is a good idea. But the controversy over seed-saving strategies begs the question of why we need all these seed banks in the first place. I asked Dan McGuire, a farm owner in Nebraska and an executive with the American Corn Growers Foundation, to comment on this from the American farmer's point of view. He said maybe the Scandinavian countries who are building the Doomsday Vault know something that we don't know. "I expect they don't place blind trust in the agribusiness biotechnology strategy to enhance and protect the world's food supply," he says, "so they're hedging their bets." That may be. No one knows how all this will turn out. Fowler says we need to embrace all forms of diversity preservation. When I asked him if the Doomsday Vault will save agriculture in the future, he smiled and said, "Well, to be modest, five hundred years from now, we'll know."

The Perfect Storm

We find ourselves at a turning point. Seeds are increasingly becoming private property, and that ownership is concentrating. Plant breeding too is being privatized and focused on one technology, genetic engineering. Seed banks are on the brink of choosing which side to favor, private interests or the small farmer. All this may be a prelude to a coming famine. That's the scenario most favored by those who believe in the botany of scarcity. And to make matters worse, all this is happening within a larger context of our worsening environmental condition. These are the elements of the perfect storm: the decreasing diversity of the world's seeds; increasing private control over seeds, agricultural technology, and plant breeding; rising populations and their increasing need for water, food, and energy; and the declining capacity of the natural world. These trends can result in famine, or worse, if they are not addressed. Or they can alert us to the need for change and stimulate public debate. As a journalist covering the environment, I believe that of all the threats to the environment—and there are many—the three most important are the acceleration of global warming, the impacts of industrial agriculture, and the rapid extinction of species. All of them are caused by human activity, all of them implicate the future of seeds, and all of them deserve our careful consideration.

Industrial agriculture is exhausting the soil, polluting the water, and stimulating overproduction and overconsumption. We have begun to eat ourselves out of our planetary house and home. And yet for all its troubles, agriculture is unique among our current environmental challenges, because while it may be the biggest problem we have created for ourselves, it is also the best opportunity we have to turn things around. Agriculture, as we will see, is full of potential solutions to the food, fuel, and biodiversity crisis. And since we're all engaged in feeding ourselves in some way, the way we eat offers all of us a meaningful opportunity to engage in environmental change. The challenge comes when we face the magnitude of the problems and try to connect the dots between them. However, this has to happen so we can know more about what the problems are, understand our role in the solutions, and participate not just in what works for us personally but in what works for the planet.

Agriculture is a system. All its parts are interconnected, and the system of agriculture connects to all the basic biological systems that maintain life on earth. Instead of looking at each issue separately, we can best understand agriculture as one part of that larger integrated system of life on earth. Looking at the whole can feel overwhelming. We are deluged with bad news every day, and both the doomsayers and the deniers are vying for our attention. Noticing a problem and then disregarding it is understandable; it can be like sorting through junk mail. But the systemic point of view is a far more powerful and useful perspective, because rather than letting one problem pile on top of another, it allows us to see how things fit together and how even small choices can make a big difference.

Energy drives industry as well as our homes and businesses, but one of the biggest energy consumers is industrial agriculture. It uses close to 20 percent of the world's energy to grow, transport, process, and distribute food. Because of its dependence on fossil-fuel-based synthetic fertilizers and pesticides, industrial agriculture uses up ten times more energy than it generates. Put another way, industrial food is nine parts oil and one part farm. Some uses are even more excessive, such as our demand for imported and out-of-season foods. Hothouse tomatoes grown in the Netherlands, for example, take 100 times more energy to produce and send to the United States than the calories they provide.

Industrial agriculture may also be the world's biggest polluter. Yale professor James Gustave Speth says that industrial agriculture uses six hundred different registered pesticides, releasing 5 to 6 billion pounds of them into the global environment every year. According to a recent U.S. Geological Survey, the 1 billion pounds of pesticides that American farmers use every year have contaminated almost all of the nation's streams and rivers, as well as the fish living in them, with toxic cancer- and birth-defect-causing chemicals.

Will Rogers had it right when he said, "They're makin' people every day, but they ain't makin' any more dirt." Actually, under ideal conditions, nature does build soil, but only at a rate of 1 inch of topsoil every five hundred years. Meanwhile the United States is losing topsoil thirteen times faster than it can be replaced. Worldwide, 5 billion acres of soil (more than the area of the United States and Canada combined) have been degraded. In India, this damage has cut agricultural productivity by almost $2.4 billion a year. In Africa, three quarters of arable land is severely degraded, worsening the hunger crisis there.

The global cost of soil erosion is estimated to be more than

$400 billion each year. This includes pollution, salinization, wind and water erosion, and overgrazing on marginal lands that are already fragile and, in semiarid places, less able to recover from overuse and contamination than other lands. China reports that 24 million acres, about one tenth of its arable land, were polluted in 2006. Meanwhile, the human population is projected to be 9 billion by 2050, with each person multiplying both consumption and the exhaustion of these resources. Much of that growth will take place in India and China.

Water is the other essential, to life and to agriculture. Industrial agriculture uses 70 percent of the earth's fresh water for irrigation. It then returns that water to rivers and lakes loaded with pollutants. Now wherever the rivers meet the ocean, they create "dead zones" where nothing grows because of the high levels of nutrients in the agricultural runoff. The UN says that the need for water could double in the next fifty years. In less than half that time, by 2025, two thirds of the world's population will live in a situation of "water stress" and 2 billion people will be living with an "absolute water shortage." In China, one quarter of the groundwater is already overdrafted, and in parts of India overdrafting is more than double that rate.

The overuse of fossil fuels, water shortages, and soil degradation are putting the brakes on the productivity of industrial agriculture everywhere. The environmental costs of industrial agriculture are not just rising; they are accumulating and multiplying. Any future incremental gains in production that rely on industrial methods will only exacerbate these problems. In other words, the real cost of doing business as usual is going up fast. As Pearce points out, we are growing "twice as much food as a generation ago, but we use three times more water to do so."

Another factor to take into consideration is land use. Only slightly more than 11 percent of the earth's surface is protected as parks or reserves. The other almost 90 percent is human-dominated, and 30 percent of that, according to the FAO, is devoted to livestock grazing and animal feed production. Then there is the growth of urbanization and its impacts on the land, resources, and wildlife. Speth's assessment looked at the result of all this economic expansion on large ecosystems and wildlife populations. He says we've lost one third to one half of the world's forests, about half the mangroves and other wetlands, 30 percent of fish species, 24 percent of mammals, and 25 percent of reptiles, as well as a fourth of all bird species.

Clearly we are headed for an inevitable confrontation between the excesses of industrial agriculture and the limits of the natural world. It's no longer a question of if this will happen but when, and how bad it will be. The United Nations issued its first environmental report card in 2005, as part of its Millennium Ecosystem Assessment project. It brought together the work of more than 1,300 ecologists and researchers from 95 countries and noted the serious deterioration of all the biological systems we depend on—soil, water, fish, forests, biodiversity. The report concluded that human activity is directly or indirectly degrading 60 percent of the earth's capacity for life support, and it singled out agriculture as one of the worst culprits. This degradation, the report also noted, was being fueled by destructive agricultural and development subsidies, incoherent government policies, and our habit of persistently treating nature as a free and disposable resource.

Stuart Pimm calculates that humans now use 42 percent of the earth's plant growth and 50 percent of the water and that the richer nations take more than their fair share of the natural productivity of the earth. Of course, that's one reason that they're rich. But Pimm's point is that this means the poor are forced to use less resilient, more marginal resources, which in turn inflicts even greater damage. And the greater injustice is about to come, because as global warming hits, it will come down on the poor first and hurt them the most.

Chicken Little Was Right

Melting glaciers, rising sea levels, and unusual weather patterns are making the headlines. But most people don't feel the effects of global environmental problems until they hit close to home. Right now rising gas prices are getting our attention. But soon the price of food will start to creep up as well. In the long run, the agricultural sector, even more than the energy sector, will be affected by global warming.

Agriculture as we know it came about as a result of warming trends that began with the end of the last two ice ages. Now another climatic shift will force us to change again, but the plants we developed over the past ten thousand years for our food have adapted to a fairly narrow spectrum of climatic conditions. Global warming will change weather patterns, make precipitation more unpredictable, and destabilize the temperature and moisture conditions that these plants rely on to grow, mature, and set seed. Heavy storms, spikes in temperatures, and unseasonable weather will disrupt crops and planting patterns.

Global warming will have a major impact on topsoil because as temperatures rise, soil moisture is lost. This is perhaps the greatest threat to all agricultural systems, both industrial and ecological. Topsoil is what feeds the plants that feed us and our animals. It's teeming with microorganisms, worms, insects, and leaf litter. There has to be sufficient moisture and the right temperature range to keep this "soil foodweb" alive. Without soil moisture, a plant's roots and vascular conveyance system cannot draw the nutrients it needs from the soil. And it is those nutrients that keep us and the rest of the planet alive.

Former vice president Al Gore predicts a 25 to 30 percent loss of soil moisture in the most valuable agricultural growing areas of the country. If nothing is done to address the problem, 60 percent of soil moisture will be lost, he says, calling inaction on this problem a "scorched earth" policy. Gore goes on to predict both floods and droughts as a result of the loss of soil moisture. As soil warms and dries, it erodes and blows away. Belowground, the network of mycelium fibers desiccates, depriving plants and trees of their invisible support system. That causes cascading effects, eventually resulting in the loss of understory plants, insects, and birds, as well as decreases in water retention and all the other "ecosystem services" that forests perform, and it accelerates deforestation. Aboveground, warmer temperatures will favor the proliferation of weeds, which are heartier than crops and some native plants.

Plants and animals are already changing their habitats. Many birds and butterflies and some plants have begun moving north. Insects are appearing in places they have never been before. Warmer winters will allow some pests to flourish where they might otherwise have been killed off by cold weather. Blooming times will shift. Pollination cycles will be unhinged as plants bloom ahead of schedule or the pollinators do not show up on time. As plants move north in response to temperature changes, they might encounter new soils that are a lot less fertile or other conditions they have not yet adapted to, and their survival will be compromised.

It has been suggested that farmers could simply shift their crops to the north. But they too will encounter different conditions, including day lengths, which determine flowering, not to mention other people who are already living there. Higher temperatures will also mean more evaporation and respiration, more heat stress, and consequently less fertility. Insect damage will increase. This will result in the use of more chemicals, with their accompanying environmental impacts. And as sea levels rise, the inundation will result in the loss of wetland rice-growing areas, greater salt intrusion, and less drainage for croplands. Sorry, there is no good news here.

Last, agriculture will be affected by rising levels of CO_2, which is a complicated but crucial matter. Plants harvest sunlight. Through the magic of photosynthesis, they use it to convert water and nutrients from the soil, along with carbon dioxide from the air, into sugars, starches, and cellulose and oxygen. As levels of CO_2 increase, plants increase their production of carbohydrates. Some crops, such as wheat and rice, are more responsive to CO_2 than others, like corn, sorghum, and sugar cane. How all this will work out in the field has not been adequately studied. What is known at this point is that rising CO_2 levels mean, in the short term, more biomass production. That may be good for the production of biofuels using plants, but it's not so good for growing food.

Simply put, the earth has a limited capacity for regeneration. Like our own bodies, the more stress it has to cope with, the less resilient it becomes. We are now appropriating 40 percent of the photosynthetic products of the plant world each year, and we are releasing more and more carbon dioxide. At some point the capacity of plants and soil to absorb CO_2 will max out and more carbon dioxide will build up in the atmosphere. That will trigger the multiplier effects of global warming and increase temperatures, which in turn will decrease the ability of plants to keep up. This is a recipe for widespread biological suicide and plays into the other crucial environmental problem we face, species extinction.

Every prognosticator on this subject says that human activity is causing the elimination of species at the rate of somewhere between one hundred and one thousand times the natural rate of extinction. It's being called "the sixth great extinction." In his book *The Future of Life,* E. O. Wilson says that one half of all species of life on earth will be gone in one hundred years. This assault on the earth's biological endowment is a planetary catastrophe of the highest order, and the difference between this and past extinctions is that this time it is caused by human activity. Species Alliance, an organization working to help people come to terms with this devastation, says that 90 percent of the world's large fish have disappeared from the oceans and populations of large animals like lions and apes are also in danger. We know much less about the smaller forms of life, especially plants.

According to experts involved in the Global Strategy for Plant Conservation, meeting under the Convention on Biological Diversity, we don't even know how many plants there are in the world, let alone how many are threatened with extinction. The number of plant species is estimated to range from about 230,000 to over 400,000. Estimates of the number of those threatened range from "over 100,000," according to Peter Raven of the

St. Louis International Botanical Garden, to the most conservative number used by the World Conservation Union's 1998 "Red List" of plant species at risk, which is about 31,000.

In May 2007, CGIAR released a report on the impacts of global warming on plant species which said that climate change threatens the extinction of many wild relatives of plants that are highly valued, such as the potato and the peanut. Losing the wild relatives of crop varieties presents plant conservationists with an extremely serious problem. CGIAR says the need to collect and store seeds of wild relatives of food plants, not just crops, is now urgent. It notes that existing collections "are conserving only a fraction of the wild species" that need to be preserved in order to protect the genetic integrity and diversity of our food crops. While CGIAR deserves credit for finally making this point, it has yet to propose any conservation strategies other than what it is already doing—ex-situ seed saving.

E. O. Wilson told Congress in 1982, when he was testifying on behalf of the Endangered Species Act, that "the worst thing that can happen during the 1980s is not energy depletion, economic collapse, limited nuclear war, or conquest by a totalitarian government. As terrible as these catastrophes would be for us, they could be repaired within a few generations. The one process, already ongoing in the 1980s, that will take millions of years to correct is the loss of genetic and species diversity by the destruction of natural habitats. This is the folly our descendants are least likely to forgive us."

One Breath, One Degree, One Decade

Jim Hansen is the director of NASA's Goddard Institute for Space Studies. He is a courageous public scientist who has been outspoken about the dangers of global warming. He became the bête noire of the Bush administration during its attempts to silence climate scientists. Hansen says we are now teetering on the edge of irrevocable change, and he is by no means alone in this assessment. Most scientists agree that we are rapidly approaching a threshold past which, if we keep on going as we are, life itself will be imperiled. Hansen says, "We may only have one decade, and one degree of warming, before the monsters are fully awake."

We have one vital breath that must be saved, the breath that the earth takes every year. As the earth wobbles on its axis, the oceans ebb and flow and the seasons change. Early climate studies revealed that this causes an annual cycling of carbon dioxide from summer to winter. In the spring, as plants and other photosynthetic organisms grow, they absorb carbon dioxide from the air. Then in the fall and winter, as they die and decay and are eaten by other organisms, they release it. As Fred Pearce so eloquently put it, "The earth, in effect, breathes in and out once a year." This breath dramatically highlights the interdependence of climate systems, the oceans, and plant systems and the need to see the world as an interconnected whole. Our lives are completely dependent on all the life cycles that maintain the living, breathing earth.

As a journalist, I am often perplexed by the lack of public concern over these environmental issues, especially since our very survival depends on their proper functioning. Some responsibility for this must fall on the mainstream media, because it cannot and do not convey the complexity and urgency of these problems. I don't think it's environmental alarmism to say that we are facing extremely serious perils. My concern is that instead of getting involved in making sure our government institutions are working in our interest and insisting on having the best publicly controlled technologies available, we will be tempted by the pain all this bad news causes to bury our heads in the sand and just hope for the best. Or, worse, we will hand over crucial decisions about our future to private interests. Unfortunately, we can't afford the luxury of denial. We have run out of time to experiment with unproven, dangerous technologies like agricultural genetic engineering.

Writing in the year 2000, scientist Bill Joy warned that the widespread use of biotechnology had an unlimited potential for destruction. He said, "I think it is no exaggeration to say we are on the cusp of the further perfection of extreme evil." He argued that genetic engineering and other new private technologies would cause more damage and not solve our problems. As he and others have pointed out, the threat comes both from these technologies themselves and from the fact that we lack the ethical and intellectual capacity to understand them and to control the way they rule our lives.

If we had another twenty or thirty years to figure out how to use these tools, and if we, the general public, had a choice and a means to do so, we might go ahead and spend some time experimenting. We could see what works and how best to use it. But we don't have that kind of time. We've lost our margin of error. We can't afford to vest our hopes, our health, and our future in ideas that are exclusively controlled by a few companies that have already proven by their past and current conduct that they do not have our best interests in mind.

What we need are proven, time-tested technologies that can be locally controlled, openly and inexpensively reproduced, and safely deployed anywhere. We need a technology that would, for instance, increase food production while nourishing the soil; purify the water; address the need for plant diversity and resiliency; preserve and restore the integrity of both natural and cultural systems; and ensure local prosperity. We already have such a technology. It's called organic farming.

SEVEN

The Botany of Abundance

I think that more knowledge of how to co-operate
with nature for our own good is the greatest need
of the world today. Man's control of his own future
may depend in the long run on whether his biological knowledge, which is constructive, can catch up
with his knowledge of the physical sciences, which
has taught him so much about how to destroy.

HENRY A. WALLACE, *secretary of
agriculture, 1937 USDA Yearbook*

Fort Collins, Colorado

A strong westward wind could kick up over the Nebraska prairie
and blow steadily across the plains without much interruption
until it hit the Front Range, the eastern flank of the Rocky Mountains. That's where the city of Fort Collins huddles up against the
foothills that gently rise to the west before becoming the high
jagged peaks of the Medicine Bow Mountains, then the Conti-
nental Divide. In the mid-nineteenth century, migrants moving
west also stopped here. They settled the lands of the Ute nation
and of other tribes, who did their best to resist the invasion. To
protect themselves from Indian retaliation, the colonists established Camp Collins in 1862 with two companies of the Kansas
Volunteer Cavalry. After the Civil War and after local hostilities
died down, the fort was taken over by a farmer from New York

named Franklin Avery. He established a private company and laid out a plan for the town of Fort Collins, modeled after the nearby agrarian community of Greeley, named for Horace "Go west, young man" Greeley.

Avery was inspired by the hard work and temperance practiced by the Greeley community, and by its prosperity. In 1879, Fort Collins used federal land grants to establish the Colorado State Agricultural and Mechanical College, which brought the latest farming technologies, irrigation, crop rotation, and mechanization to the area. Today Colorado State University is still an aggie school. The main buildings along College Avenue are built of yellow brick with red tile roofs and are placed in the center of large grassy lawns, as if to say that there's plenty of water and land around these parts.

Driving to Fort Collins today is another experience altogether. The trip from Denver takes about an hour, using the fast toll road from the new airport and then heading north on Interstate 25. Development along this highway corridor has erased the dreams of the early immigrants. The seventy-mile-an-hour view is of a Wal-Martian landscape of urban sprawl. There are a few scattered farms left, many of them sprouting rocking-horse oil pumps in their fields, but the billboards announce more development for the future. The stench of animal confinement and feeding operations gives away their presence, but it's mostly the people confinement and feeding operations of modern subdivisions and malls. The Colorado Visitor Center offers free coffee, maps, and racks of colorful brochures praising Fort Collins as a vacation wonderland. It's that dual reality of the West: behind the tilt-up front of gorgeous scenery, there's a wasteland.

The town of Fort Collins is unremarkable, except for the old section where the college is located. In a nondescript building behind the track field is the National Seed Storage Laboratory. Inside, slumbering in cold storage, is our nation's most important collection of seeds. The official name for this facility is the National Center for Genetic Resources Preservation, part of the larger U.S. National Plant Germplasm System (NPGS), a complicated network of twenty sites that includes laboratories, introduction stations, specialized repositories, and gene banks. NPGS also manages crop-specific centers for potatoes in Wisconsin, grapevines in Davis, California, apples in Geneva, New York, and tropical crops in Florida and Hawai'i.

Fort Collins is a state-of-the-art gene bank and one of the world's top seed preservation and research facilities. It houses the nation's "base collection" of 475,000 samples from 6,000 different species, as well as a safety backup collection of 230,000 samples from the CGIAR centers. It uses two large walk-in freezers, one for very-low-temperature short-term storage, at minus 5 degrees centigrade, and the other for long-term storage at minus 18 degrees. The heavy steel doors with rubber seals slide open with a loud *whoosh,* and suddenly the air is full of freezing vapors, a harsh white light, and the sound of fans roaring. The insides are lined with steel racks stacked from floor to ceiling. Hundreds of seed samples are arranged on the shelves in paper envelopes and foil bags; others are held in long thin plastic tubes, all bar-coded and labeled.

There are basically two types of seeds, those that are called "orthodox," which means they can be dried and stored for long periods, and those called "recalcitrant," which means they need to be kept at a higher moisture level and cannot be frozen. Some plant and animal materials are kept in cryogenic storage in a room full of squat stainless steel tanks used to store seed, meristems, buds of plants that do not reproduce by seed, and animal semen, blood, and embryos. When the top comes off one of these small rotund tanks, a fog of liquid nitrogen leaks out and slinks down the sides, like a witch's cauldron spilling over.

The seed vaults at Fort Collins are housed in a separate building within the main building. It was built with heavy thick walls and has elaborate electronic security. The large main storage vault is the most impressive. It's kept very cold and dry and is full of massive movable floor-to-ceiling racks that slide along on tracks, like the ones used by libraries. Each shelf holds thousands of cataloged samples of seeds. To some, this is a living library. Others think of Fort Collins as the Fort Knox of seeds. To me, it felt more like being in church. It was a surprisingly deep and moving experience. There are almost a million seed samples stored here. Each seed is a messenger from another time and place, waiting patiently while slowly dying, enshrouded in a bag and kept dormant with the best available twenty-first-century preservation technology.

Seed saving and collecting in North America began informally. George Washington and Thomas Jefferson considered seed saving essential to establishing a stable economy for the nation. Native Americans had their own seed-saving practices, both from wild harvests and farming, and they grew far more kinds of food and medicinal plants than colonists did. The early settlers would have starved if the native planters had not shared their seeds. North America had few native plants easily used for food—just the sunflower and some berries and nuts. Even the staples used by Native Americans, like corn, beans, squash, tomatoes, potatoes, chilies, and even cotton, came from somewhere else.

Seeds have always accompanied people on their migrations. The agriculture we have today is based on seeds brought into the country by explorers, the military, immigrants, and slaves. The first botanical collection was founded in 1842, when greenhouses were built in Washington, D.C. The U.S. Patent Office was in charge of plant collections, and it purchased, inspected, and repackaged seeds, which were given to members of Congress to send to constituents, using their free postage privileges. By 1861, almost 2.5 million packages of seed were being distributed through members of Congress every year. Throughout most of the nineteenth century, the federal government provided free, high-quality seed to farmers and gardeners.

In 1862, President Lincoln established the Department of Agriculture, in part to collect, propagate, and distribute seeds and to breed plants. He called it "the people's department." The new USDA took over seed distribution and established a nationwide network of colleges, the land-grant universities, charging them with plant breeding and research. For the next fifty years, agriculture prospered from a workable combination of the abundant natural fertility of the nation's soil, the hard work of farmers, and government support for seed saving and plant breeding. Plantation agriculture, founded on slave labor, formed the basis of the industrial model, but until later in the twentieth century, most farming was done by a decentralized system of independent family farmers. Then, in a complete reversal of fortune, by the end of the twentieth century agriculture in American was almost entirely industrialized. There are now more people in prison than there are farmers in America.

There'll Always Be Another Aphid

In his book *First the Seed*, sociologist Jack Kloppenburg tells the history of how plants and seeds were bred and distributed in the United States. As late as 1878, he says, a third of the USDA's annual budget was still devoted to seed collection and free distribution. There wasn't much systematic plant breeding until 1898, when the USDA started the Section of Seed and Plant Introduction. Then professional botanists began breeding plants for improved traits and disease resistance. This in turn stimulated more plant collecting, and a list was started to keep track of all the new introductions. Each plant was given a "plant introduction number." PI Number One on this Inventory of Foreign Seeds and Plants was a cabbage variety introduced from Russia in 1898.

The public investment in plant collecting, breeding, and seed distribution paid off handsomely, but it was not to last. Soon the USDA began to fall under the shadow of private interests. The secretary of agriculture in 1893 was J. Sterling Morton, a conservative who said that the government's free seed program was infringing on "the rights of citizens engaged in legitimate trade pursuits." A nascent seed industry had begun to organize as the American Seed Trade Association (ASTA). At first members of Congress resisted the effort to end the government seed program because they didn't want to give up their popular freebie. In 1897, a record 22 million packages, each one containing five packets of various seeds—1 billion seed packets—were sent out. This was very high quality cleaned and tested seed. The same cannot be said about the products offered by private companies. As Kloppenburg points out, "it is no accident" that the first thing ASTA did at its inaugural meeting was adopt a disclaimer for its seed packages, "repudiating responsibility for the performance of their product."

At the beginning of the twentieth century, American agriculture was rich and prosperous, but soon the USDA began to bloat. In 1903, it started to build its headquarters in Washington, D.C.: a massive, intimidating, and impenetrable six-story labyrinth of offices and hallways fronted by a 650-foot-long classical façade. The policy changes instituted by the USDA began a long, steady decline in the economic independence of the American farmer. When farmers got seed for free or saved their own, they could re-plant it, exchange it, or sell it as another source of income. Once they had to purchase seed, it was a small step for purveyors to include other products, like fertilizers and pesticides, and end the on-farm production of the means of farming. Soon farmers got hooked on credit, and a midcentury secretary of agriculture told them to "get big or get out." By 2006, the USDA's budget had swollen to $94.6 billion, with most of the money going to mandatory programs like food stamps and to support agribusiness.

Economist Chuck Benbrook found that as early as the mid-1980s, as the seed/pesticide industry consolidated, the price of farm inputs rose and growers began realizing lower returns. At the same time private companies began investing in plant-breeding efforts, and the budgets of the nation's seed banks, botanical gardens, and plant-breeding programs began to stagnate or fall. When Jack Doyle wrote about the Fort Collins facility in *Altered Harvest* in 1985, he remarked about the fact that it was located "on an earthquake fault . . . roughly equidistant between a nuclear power plant and the Rocky Flats plutonium facility . . . not exactly the Rock of Gibraltar." Doyle called attention to the need for better funding for the facility and said that the collections there were vulnerable to decay, neglect, and even the possibility of viral infections.

All public seed banks are vulnerable, as we have seen. But there's no question about the value of the materials they hold and the research they perform. And while I would prefer to see on-farm breeding and widely dispersed seed-saving networks, I am not about to give up on our public seed banks. NPGS, like many USDA agencies, is full of dedicated, public-service-minded people. If it were up to them, the nation's crop diversity would be in good hands. If they and the great land-grant system of colleges and universities could be held to their mission of public-interest research and the public was willing to support these institutions, American agriculture could return to a "botany of abundance" through public plant breeding.

Time and again public seed banks have been called on to save a crop when it gets hit with disease or drought. When southern corn leaf blight swept the nation's corn fields in the 1970s and the Russian wheat aphid ruined crops in the 1990s, the genes stored in the facility at Fort Collins and at CIMMYT in Mexico came to the rescue. Still, there will always be another aphid, probably one that's even more lethal than the last one. When the next one comes, the ability of NPGS to respond appropriately (in the public interest) depends on three things: what's in the collection, whether what's there is characterized (its attributes described) and can be located, and whether it can be kept in the public domain.

One hundred and ten years after the USDA plant introduction system began, the public's collection has little left from its first fifty years: only about 50,000 samples. Less than 20 percent of that material was ever characterized. Most of the varieties that were distributed by the government in the nineteenth century are now gone. Dave Ellis, a curator and lead scientist at Fort Collins, says that the staff can hardly keep up with the current inventory, let alone find something collected in the distant past. He said they recently got a request for a 1903 acquisition, and after days of searching, they finally found information about it in an old book they happened on by accident. In *The Last Harvest,* Paul Raeburn says that Fort Collins represents "the accumulated wisdom of hundreds of years of crop domestication and improvement by farmers around the world" and that the NPGS is responsible for billions of dollars of agricultural value, but it only gets about $30 million a year, an amount "too small to rate the status of a separate line in the department's budget."

Five thousand varieties of corn were sent to Fort Collins in the 1960s as a backup collection. Years later, when budget woes at CIMMYT in Mexico nearly forced a shutdown of that facility, some of its samples were lost as well. Researchers at CIMMYT were counting on the backup collection at Fort Collins, but somehow it had disappeared. Major Goodman, one of the world's leading authorities on corn, is quoted by Raeburn as saying that if he had known the materials were being discarded by Fort Collins, which is what was reported, he could have stopped it. Goodman told me that neither he nor any other corn expert was consulted about those corn varieties and that thousands of corn samples have been lost because of confusion and poor safekeeping by seed banks in the United States and Mexico.

As for the lost backup collection, Henry Shands, who until 2007 was the director of the Fort Collins facility, says he looked into it and concluded that "no material was ever discarded." Shands found correspondence requesting the return of the material, which indicates that it was returned to CIMMYT. He says it "probably sat unceremoniously on the shelf to be discarded there, before or after it died." Shands says the staff at Fort Collins did a complete inventory when they built a new vault in 1991, and "other material I was seeking did not appear then, and that troubles me more than the maize." Goodman says that what's constraining these "honorable, hardworking folks" is a lack of resources, but so much of what has been collected has been lost, and that's because no one knows what it is or what to do with it. Every seed-preservation expert interviewed for this book emphasized the importance of these management problems and noted how they contribute to the loss of plant diversity.

The ETC Group studied seventy-five kinds of vegetables that were on old USDA lists and found that 97 percent of them were extinct. Of the 2,683 pear varieties, 87.7 percent are now extinct. Also 578 varieties of beets, 434 varieties of field corn and 307 of sweet corn, 285 varieties of cucumber, 497 varieties of lettuce, 408 varieties of tomato, and dozens of every other kind of seed plant from asparagus to watermelon are gone. And these extinctions were tabulated before the worst ravages of industry consolidation, industrial agriculture, and patented seed technologies began.

Nazreen Kadir says that gene collections themselves can contribute to the narrowing of diversity. "When you start collecting," she explains, "it means you have to select. And when you start to select and intentionally propagate only certain species, that is a march towards concentration." She makes an important point, because as things stand now, we have less and less to work with. When plant breeding was part of community farm life, farmers in each locality could select and adapt the plants that did best for them. As local and public plant-breeding efforts fade and as corporations take over, the way plants are selected and used for breeding changes. Now plant breeding is done with computers and genetic databases, micro-arrays, and DNA chips that can be mixed and matched. This has sped up the process dramatically, but it's expensive, selective, and generally proprietary, a process that appears to increase the privatization of a germplasm. Agribusiness giant Pioneer says, "We've spent decades and billions of dollars developing the world's largest plant genetics library. We will vigorously protect it, as we always have."

In 2005, Henry Shands coauthored an impassioned call for protecting the nation's seed collections called "Safeguarding the Future of U.S Agriculture." He warned that the public seed-saving sector was being taken for granted and that there was an assumption that the private gene banks would "ensure food security now and in the future." Although "the biggest firms do have impressive gene banks," he said that they "tend to focus on only a handful of major crops." He cited an Agricultural Research Source (ARS) study that found that while research and development increased fourteenfold between 1960 and 1996, it "concentrated on corn, soybeans and cotton." Meanwhile, public plant breeding was "more likely to benefit a greater variety of more 'minor' crops."

Shands's report said we need to "be prepared for the unknown," which may take the form of a "mutated fungus" or other pathogen, and the answers are in the world's public gene collections. Other historians of the decline of public breeding programs are more alarmed. Mary Hendrickson at the University of Missouri says that the balance of power has shifted to the private realm, which is now controlled by five or six clusters of private interests. Private research devotes $5 billion a year to finding newer and more effective chemicals. Meanwhile, the natural world keeps finding ways to outsmart them. The industry thinks it can win its war on bugs, but the aphids are too clever.

At the same time, science has begun to validate the pest-control methods used by organic farmers, who take biological realities into account and have apparently worked out a peace treaty with bugs. Even the USDA has taken notice. After many years of neglecting the intellectual infrastructure of sustainable agriculture, the USDA has begun funding organic research. In 2005, it devoted about $10 million to the topic, which is encouraging, but it is not very much considering that the overall research budget for USDA is $2 billion.

Henry Shands spent most of his career at the USDA. He's an avuncular man, bald, with a strong build and a quietly reassuring manner—just the type of person you'd want to be in charge of your most precious possessions. He seemed wistful during several interviews at Fort Collins, and at the end of a long day he walked me out to the parking lot. He paused and picked up a dried seedpod dropped by a locust tree near the entrance to the building. It rattled as he lifted his arm and pointed to the sunset. He looked like a native elder about to call out a prayer, but he was just pointing out an interesting cloud formation on the horizon. As a public official, he had been careful in his critique, but outside, at the end of the day, he was more reflective. He said he regretted the loss of expertise in the public system and the people who knew plants personally, passionately. It was the same thing Cary Fowler had said about the need for people who fall in love with a crop, someone like the great corn geneticist Barbara McClintock, who, it's said, had "a feeling for the organism." What Shands did not say was that he too was leaving this work. Just a few months later he was gone, and his cluttered office at Fort Collins was left empty.

Handing Out White Hats

This history provides the backdrop for the real melodrama, which is how all these changes in policy, and changes in the lives of the people who built the great public system, affect agriculture. Right now our public policy has capitulated to industry, leaving the future of seeds in private hands. The lady tied to the tracks in our melodrama is the public research system and public seed collections. Congress and the USDA, having abandoned their obligation to protect this priceless public trust, are standing aside. Meanwhile, the real villain, industry, lets out a menacing laugh. The train that is headed our way is the decline of plant genetic diversity. Will the guys in the black hats and their sidekicks with the badges save the day? Not likely.

The person who plays the role of Dudley Do-Right for coming to the rescue of American agriculture is Wes Jackson. Thirty years ago, Jackson founded the Land Institute in Salina, Kansas. Its mission statement says, "When people, land, and community are as one, all three members prosper; when they relate not as members but as competing interests, all three are exploited. By consulting nature as the source and measure of the membership, the Land Institute seeks to develop an agriculture that will save soil from being lost or poisoned while promoting a community life at once prosperous and enduring." It's as good a definition of sustainable agriculture as there can be, and the work of the Land Institute is the best there is. Jackson's countless articles, books, and lectures and work at the institute have reoriented a whole generation of farmers and environmental advocates to the idea of farming in the image of nature.

Jackson has a love of science matched only by his love for a good turn of phrase. He took a small part of the Kansas prairie that had been spared the predations of sod busting and began working on a radical idea: designing a plant community that would produce like a farm field but act like a prairie. The Land Institute began its work by looking at the deeply rooted native grasses, which are self-fertilizing, self-weeding, drought-tolerant, and continuously productive. Not a bad idea for a farm. The secret strategy used by these grasses is diversity. Years ago they welcomed in all their plant cousins and, as a plant community, figured out which ones would respond to varying conditions and then alternated their responsibilities. When it's dry, the shorter grasses are called on to work. Others do better when pests arrive. Like a forest, the prairie grows enough different kinds of plants with the right combination of structures and metabolisms to survive as a whole community, not necessarily as individuals.

All healthy plant communities live by the ancient principle "as above, so below." Most of the action takes place underground. The Land Institute's most famous poster is a photograph of the roots of an annual crop grass, which appear short and stunted and only a few inches long, placed next to the roots of a native prairie grass, gracefully dangling down several feet. Perennial grains make a tradeoff between what they produce above and what goes on below, compromising the seed output in favor of the root system. The institute's goal is to increase aboveground yield without losing hardiness. It does this by imitating nature and planting perennial crops in polycultures.

If this system were used to grow grains and forage, it would virtually eliminate many of the wounds of industrial agriculture by eliminating machine-caused soil loss and the use of chemicals. Plus it would increase biodiversity. The institute's basic research has already worked out many useful ideas, all documented in scientific papers. Its staff members are building a body of knowledge and a wider community of researchers who are committed to this vision. When asked about how plant breeding is changing and why all the attention is now on industry, Jackson digs into his bag of favorite stories and comes out with the one about the drunk who is searching for his keys under the streetlamp. A passerby asks him why he is looking there, since he lost the keys somewhere else, and the drunk replies, "Yeah, I know, but the light here is better."

The Land Institute is thirty years into its fifty-year agenda to return agriculture to its natural roots. "If you want quick, cut-rate science," Jackson says, speaking like the geneticist he is, "this isn't for you, because it's going to take decades to shuffle the chromosomes. Oh, we'll have something promising in twenty-five years that will energize us. Sorghum and wheat will come first, corn and soybeans later." It's the long time frame that may be the prairie's most enduring lesson for agriculture, and Jackson knows he is taking on a 10,000-year-old problem.

Salina, Kansas, is a small town located smack in the middle of the United States. It quietly shimmers in the summer heat, with only the mournful sound of a train whistle fading into the distance. Life here feels resilient even after years of drought. These communities in Middle America used to depend on industrial agriculture, but it let them down. Can little guys like the Land Institute succeed where the big guys failed? As I stand on a bit of unplowed prairie near the institute, in the middle of shoulder-high grasses sizzling with the sounds of insects and birds, it sure sounds like Jackson has nature's vote.

The other white hat award goes to another farm-based plant breeder in the Midwest, Laura Krouse, who grows organic food and breeds open-pollinated corn seed while surrounded by America's "green desert" of corn and soybeans—quite a challenge for someone living in the midst of GMO corn country. When she walks through her fields, her evident love of corn shows in the way she touches her plants. She picks off a tiny embryonic ear of corn, leans over it, and, using her fingers to spread it apart, talks excitedly about all its tiny parts and what they can do. Krouse was trained as a biologist and still teaches in the public land-grant system, but her heart is on her farm in southeastern Iowa. Her corn seed goes back to a man named Burt Neal, who went to the 1903 World Corn Exposition and brought back kernels from the winning ears. It has grown on this farm ever since. Krouse bought the seed along with the land.

Krouse is working on how many plants per acre she can get away with planting. She says, "It turns out that what gave hybrid corn its yield advantage is not so much that the ears were so much bigger or the kernels were heavier but that the plants tolerated more density, so farmers could plant more per acre." Krouse grows her certified organic corn as animal feed, along with food crops for dozens of families from her large organic market garden and community-supported agriculture cooperative. She has to make sure that she times the planting and pollinating of her corn just right to avoid its contamination by her neighbors, and she constantly tests it. A few years ago, GMO contamination cost her both her organic certification and half her business. She points to the feed corn growing across the road and says, "The best that corn can do is 7.8 to 8 percent protein." Her corn produces 10.5 percent protein or better, and, she says, it has a better combination of amino acids. Many of her customers run organic dairies, and they tell her that they call the chopped and fermented corn "cow candy" because their cows like it so much.

Emergence

Like Jackson and Krouse, an amazing number of people are involved in creating sustainable food systems today. It is happening all over the world, and local agriculture is growing at an astounding pace. In his book *Blessed Unrest*, social visionary and author Paul Hawken says there is an emerging social movement that until now has been largely unaware of itself. For several years Hawken has tabulated who is working on what, and he has ended up creating a remarkable new database. It's called WISER, which stands for World Index of Social and Environmental Responsibility. It divides up its listings into areas of focus. The total number of those listed who are working on issues related to food and farming, as of spring 2007, is over 7,100—that's organizations, not individuals. Another 5,436 are working on food and nourishment, 7,369 on water, 3,300 on biodiversity, over 2,366 on forestry, almost 5,000 on sustainable business and economics, and many thousands more on an array of environmental issues, the arts, peace, human rights, education, religion, ecology, and sustainability in general. Given WISER's remarkable work, it's no longer possible to think about the future without acknowledging what is going right and how numerous and connected all those engaged in change actually are, as well as the enormous potential they represent.

Still, a few more agricultural pioneers deserve to be mentioned. Lundberg Family Farms, founded by three brothers and their parents who came to California in the 1930s, decided about twenty years ago to stop using chemicals and begin to grow organic rice. Bryce Lundberg, now the third generation to manage the business, says that the farm extension service at UC was then (and largely still is) oriented to the needs of the conventional growers. So the Lundbergs had to develop their own rice varieties. Like the Straus family in Marin County, one of the earliest dairies to go organic, the Lundbergs had to figure out for themselves how to farm, and their new methods were often risky. The Lundberg and Straus families were early innovators in organic farming, but like thousands of other farmers who have come along since, they are beacons of change. And they not only became economically and environmentally successful but also made a major contribution toward developing the intellectual framework for sustainable agriculture.

Every October at the Marin Center, in San Rafael, California, in an auditorium designed by another organic visionary, Frank Lloyd Wright, thousands of people gather for the annual foot-stomping, cheering revival meeting of the new sustainability movement, the Bioneers Conference. Bioneers, named because they see themselves as "biological pioneers," was founded by

Kenny Ausubel and Nina Simons. Their conferences, books, and radio series have been a vital catalyst for innovation in food and farming as well as the sustainability movement. They've featured an array of some of the most important change agents of our time, including Fritjof Capra, educator David Orr, singer Bernice Johnson Reagon, Amory Lovins, Danny Glover and Belvie Rooks, feminist Susan Griffin, Bill McKibben, green architect Bill McDonough, and Code Pink's Jodie Evans, along with Native American farmers, Hawaiian chanters, poets, artists, reformed gang members, and scientists, all in conversation with thousands of teachers, preachers, farmers, and activists, every single one of whom is working on practical solutions for "restoration from the heart of nature."

If there is a founding mother of the new nature-based technologies movement, it has to be science writer Janine Benyus. Her book *Biomimicry* identified the "true biotechnology" revolution, which is the use of technology based in real, not artificial, biology. Benyus is brilliant at finding and describing design ideas that solve human and environmental problems. They include using snail slime as a model for lubricants, employing the light-reflecting properties of butterfly wings instead of toxic dyes to make color, and utilizing plants and fungi as living recycling systems and to detoxify waste dumps, as well as mimicking the tricks of insects like the Namibian fog beetle, which collects water droplets on its textured back. Nets have been designed that can serve the same purpose, supplying water as well as shelter in refugee camps. Benyus says that this is not the old "heat, beat, and treat" method of forcing nature into manufacturing processes. This is real creativity, the best of what the human imagination and the genius of the natural world, combined, have to offer.

Real creativity, says psychologist Rollo May, requires maturity. He says that while moral courage might help us in the righting of wrongs, real creative courage—the discovery of new forms and new patterns on which to build a new society—involves the highest level of emotional health. To that I would add that admitting that nature has already found elegant and efficient solutions to most of our problems, and that nature can guide us in our own search for ingenuity, involves a certain amount of humility. We are living in extraordinary times, given the environmental challenges we face and the paucity of solutions on offer by the titans of industry and the techno-elites. They always have been and always will be focused on their own interests. What's changed is that so many people think our public institutions are no longer viable and that all we have is the marketplace to turn to for inspiration. As a result, many of us are living by proxy, having given over all our needs to the commercial sector to meet, even our need for knowledge and creativity. It may be, as longshoreman-philosopher Eric Hoffer said, that "in times of profound change, the learners inherit the earth, while the learned find themselves beautifully equipped to deal with a world that no longer exists." Or it may be that despite the uncertainties, despite the perils, we choose to reengage.

A Green Wealth

EIGHT

Ripe for Change

Now, in the midst of so much unnecessary
human and ecological destruction, we are
facing the necessity of a new start in agriculture.

WENDELL BERRY

Heritage Farm, Decorah, Iowa

In midsummer, the softly undulating hills of northeastern Iowa
are lush with corn and soybeans. The Amish farms are immacu-
late. The town of Decorah is also orderly, a legacy of the Norwegian immigrants who began farming here in the mid-nineteenth
century. It has a real Main Street and fanciful Victorian houses
surrounded by tall trees and well-kept lawns. Just north of town
is Heritage Farm, the home of Seed Savers Exchange (SSE). Getting there means driving through mile after mile of monotonous
commodity crops, but once the road leaves the main highway, another landscape appears. The road dips down into a riparian forest and crosses a creek edged by limestone cliffs and century-old
white pine trees. The warm air suddenly turns cool, and the contrast between the planted and native riparian areas is startling. It
signals more changes to come, just over the horizon.

When you turn onto the dirt drive leading into Heritage
Farm, suddenly a circus of color appears. The summer gardens
are blazing with orange calendulas, golden sunflowers, red-
jewel-colored zinnias, white and purple coreopsis, tall spires of

pink hollyhocks and belled foxgloves, and pale, droopy-leafed coneflowers. The herb gardens are leafed in silver, purple, and maroon. Even the leaves of carefully planted rows of corn are tinged rosy pink. The farm's famous 'Grandpa Ott's' morning glory, a deep blue cup with a magenta star in the center, crawls up strings tacked onto the sides of a red barn. Color has found a home here. Even more remarkable, this impressive show is only a hint of what grows on this 860-acre farm, where SSE is doing some of the most important plant preservation work in the nation, maybe even in the world.

It all began, as so many great things do, with a gift. In 1972, Diane Whealy's grandfather gave her some seeds that her great-grandparents had brought with them from Bavaria. One was a morning glory named for her grandfather, Baptist John Ott. Those first seeds sent Diane and her husband, Kent Whealy, on a search for other heirloom plants. In 1975 their collection became Seed Savers Exchange, and since then they've distributed over 1 million rare garden seeds, their farm has expanded several times, and their membership has grown to over 7,000. Heritage Farm has a visitor center and holds conferences in a cathedral-like barn built by local Amish carpenters. It's an oak post-and-beam structure with long curved exposed ribs cradling the upstairs meeting hall. Inside, it feels like being in an upside-down ship. The lower floor serves as a large seed cleaning and sorting facility, with long tables and sinks and dozens of stainless steel sieves dangling from pegs lining the walls.

Demonstration gardens surround the well-kept buildings. Paths weave around and through raised beds where ten different kinds of corn and dozens of vegetables, herbs, flowers, and beans working their way up bamboo poles are grown. Each plant is marked with its name, and a few scattered signs tell some of their stories. One deep-red-leafed beet, developed by a Swede, is the source of the only red food coloring approved in Sweden. SSE's 35 certified organic gardens grow 500 different kinds of tomatoes and beans, 125 peppers, 1,000 varieties of peas, and many other plants. SSE offers seeds from about 650 of them in its annual seed catalog.

Only a small part of what Whealy calls the "living museum" is on public display. The rest is a collection of gardens and orchards separated by wide expanses of grass, which isolate pollinating plants; small hand-planted test plots; and machine-planted fields. There are root cellars, greenhouses, temperature-controlled storage rooms, and freezers, where the constant work of seed saving goes on all year. More than 80 percent of the 7,000 named varieties of apples that were known in the United States in 1900 are now gone. Fortunately, SSE's Historic Orchards grows 700 rare varieties of apples, most of what remains. SSE also grows 25,000 endangered varieties of historic vegetables, fruits, herbs, and flowers, including 4,000 traditional varieties from eastern Europe, 5,500 kinds of tomatoes, 1,100 kinds of peas, and over 1,000 lettuces.

Maintaining such a valuable collection is no easy task. Rare plants have to be hand-pollinated. In the greenhouse, the spindly vines of a melon that was grown from the few seeds available is watched carefully. When they mature, the male and female parts are marked with colored tape. The male flower is opened and the pollen is dabbed by hand onto the female flower. The pollinated flower is then taped shut to ensure that other pollen does not intrude. Hopefully, this kind of attention will result in more seed. SSE grows out 10 percent of its collection each year, on a ten-year rotation. But every year its catalog has a few entries marked "CROP FAILURE," a constant reminder of the challenges of saving seed.

Author Gary Paul Nabhan, who was speaking at SSE's annual meeting in 2006, said, "There are stories embedded in each of the names of each of the seeds that we grow. It's not just about saving the seeds, or the rare breeds, or the wild plants; it's about bringing those stories back so we can remember what our country is built on, what it's being sustained by, what feeds us every day." The *SSE Yearbook* is almost 500 pages long and lists all the plant material its members save, from amaranth to zucchini. It can be read as a kind of narrative of the nation, the story of American agriculture written in seed. There's the 'Lazy Housewife Bean,' the first stringless bean, introduced in 1810; the tiny black Cherokee 'Trail of Tears' bean; an unpronounceable 'Calabaza de Castukka—Ixmiquilpan Creollo' squash from Mexico, which is "resistant to everything including alkaline soil and salinity." There are hundreds of dent, flint, pop, flour, and sweet corns, with names like 'Seneca Blue Bear Dance,' 'Bloody Butcher,' and 'Mandan Bride.' Nabhan's favorite seed name belongs to a tiny bean he was given by a Southwest Indian tribe, whose name he translated as "little-bitty kitty titties."

America's agriculture is almost entirely made up of crops imported from elsewhere. For thousands of years, North America depended on a few native plants and the corn, beans, chilies, and squash that made their way north from Mesoamerica. During the early years of the nation, the Patent Office sponsored plant-collecting expeditions all over the world, adding to what the colonists brought in from Europe. As immigrants poured in, they often arrived with seeds in their pockets. Author Patricia Klindienst says that seeds and gardens provided them with living links to their former lives. She writes, "When the human community failed them, the community of the land did not. The garden is where they have claimed, or reclaimed, a just and good relationship to the earth [and] a sense of who they are and where they come from." As the twentieth century progressed, American agriculture turned toward the monotony of commodity crops and the industrial one-size-fits-all approach replaced the ingenuity of the farmer as a plant breeder. As a result, 95 percent of the cabbages, 91 percent of the field corn, 94 percent of the peas, 86 percent of the apples, and 81 percent of the tomato varieties were lost, according to the Global Crop Diversity Trust. How will plant diversity survive in this increasingly monochromatic world?

The New Agrarians

The roots of the organic farming movement go back to the early twentieth century, when Sir Albert Howard and Rudolf Steiner began warning farmers about the dangers of using chemicals and the importance of soil fertility. Ever since, alternative agriculture has been called many things—sustainable, organic, even foolish —but until recently it was always considered somewhat experimental. That changed in the 1970s, when the "back to the land" ethic created a new generation of people who wanted to grow their own food. Their values included using organic growing methods, maintaining a deep appreciation for ecological principles and aesthetics, honoring honest work and the skill of artisans, focusing on the local, and being creative and communal in their problem solving. Attention to these core values is still the hallmark of the new, and highly successful, food and farming movement.

Change in food and farming is happening so rapidly that it has spawned its own literature. Books like Eric Schlosser's *Fast Food Nation* and Michael Pollan's *Omnivore's Dilemma* have taken up permanent residency on the bestseller lists. Pollan has written numerous smart, funny, palatable articles in the *New York Times,* educating the public about eating. His work on the "cornification" of agriculture showed us how eating a burger and drinking a soda for lunch amounts to eating some corn with your corn. Nutritionist Marion Nestle has tracked the public's increasing alarm over the health problems caused by the food industry in her books *Food Politics* and *What to Eat.* The public is becoming increasingly concerned about diet-related problems like obesity, diabetes, heart disease, the health risks of pesticides, and the soaring costs of health care. The USDA estimates that simply eating a healthier diet would prevent $71 billion a year in health-care expenses.

Children are the most vulnerable. In *Food Fight,* Daniel Imhoff points out that the USDA spends $7 billion a year on a school lunch program designed to dispose of surplus commodities, not to provide nourishing food to children. Meanwhile, the food industry spends $15 billion per year on marketing snack foods, soda pop, and other dietary monstrosities to children. This food industry also happens to be the main beneficiary of the $26 billion a year that the U.S. government pays to support the very commodities that are causing these health problems, not to mention enormous environmental harm. Economically, subsidies result in dumping crops on third world countries and displacing their farmers. Worldwide, so much money is spent on production subsidies—by one estimate, over $90 billion a year—that a cow in the EU gets $2.60 a day in support while most of the world's poor still live on less than $2 a day.

Trade issues are also driving change in agriculture. New Zealand revitalized its agriculture by ending subsidies completely and banning the commercial use of GMOs. Some countries are experimenting with "green payments," subsidies that pay farmers to conserve soil, water, and biodiversity. Instead of creating a vibrant agricultural economy, farm economies that are highly subsidized are failing. At the same time, alternative and organic agriculture have achieved an unprecedented level of success, without subsidies and despite efforts by industry to frustrate their growth.

Organic food sales have expanded 20 percent a year for most of the past decade. Sales in the United States reached $25 billion in 2006. The growing demand for organic food continues to outpace supply, now that grocers like Safeway, Trader Joe's, and Wal-Mart stock organic food and natural food chains like Whole Foods are expanding. Internationally, an estimated 75 million acres of certified organic farmland are in production. Over 4,000 farmers' markets are providing Americans with a place to gather and buy fresh local food. Chefs, farm-to-school programs, Slow Food, and thousands of other local initiatives are engaged in what Alice Waters calls "the delicious revolution," which is revitalizing rural communities and changing the way America eats.

A Green Wealth

All these new agrarians need seeds. They need organic, open-pollinated, non-GMO, and heritage seeds. Companies like Snow's, Renee's Garden Seeds, and Seeds of Change are growing as the demand for these seeds increases. Over one hundred seed companies in the United States have signed the "safe seed pledge," which promises to protect diversity and the life in soil, plants, farms, and communities by making sure the seeds are free of genetically engineered organisms. Community gardens are holding local seed swaps, and groups like the Organic Seed Alliance are supporting organic seed research, production, and grower education. Like SSE, the alliance distributes seed to the needy both at home and internationally. The growth in organics is also renewing interest in plant-breeding programs that support sustainable farming and crop diversity.

As the economic and ecological advantages of farming sustainably become more apparent, mainstream farmers are also adopting practices like no-till cultivation and cover cropping. Recent research shows that nature-based pest and weed controls can be just as effective as toxic pesticides. So as chemicals become more expensive and less effective, more farmers are turning to biological techniques. This trend is bound to continue as energy prices rise. One third of the energy used by industrial agriculture goes to the production of fertilizer and pesticides. And like trade and health, energy issues are driving change in agriculture, for better or worse.

Turning plants into energy factories is not the answer to America's need for fuel. In March 2007, the Energy Department announced that it would invest $385 million in cellulosic ethanol production, a method that uses crop waste and other sources instead of food crops like corn to produce biofuel. In general, biofuels take about as much energy to produce as they yield, but that ratio is even worse for cellulosic ethanol. Commodity farming cannot replace oil with plants without raising the existing environmental and social costs exponentially. The Institute for Local

Self-Reliance says that we would have to produce seven times the amount of plant matter, in addition to what we now use for food and fiber, to meet all of our energy needs with biofuels. All plant-based biofuel strategies threaten food security and the economic livelihood of subsistence farmers. As the economic and environmental costs of food rise, the demand that biofuels will place on agriculture will exacerbate these problems.

Agriculture can become an energy supplier, but only if policies and practices are reformulated to take advantage of conservation strategies and efficiencies and use green technologies that are locally owned. Sustainable alternative energy production is already being proved, for example, by dairies that use methane digesters to provide energy to run the farm and take care of a nasty waste problem at the same time. Wind turbines are sprouting up all over fields of perennial grasses that are used both to feed animals and to provide a sustainable source of cellulose. Other farms use open areas for solar arrays that feed electricity to nearby communities. This multifunctional approach is the key, although public investment in research and development must go toward public open-source research, not private technology. If we have learned anything from the success of the local and organic food movement, it's that grassroots change is possible and transformative.

Research on model farms shows that they can produce all the energy they need for food production by using biogas generators, wind power, solar power, and fuel from farm waste, and they can provide energy to the grid as well. If these technologies were given a fraction of the billions being invested in ethanol, their enormous potential could be realized. Just as the end of oil does not mean the end of energy, the same is true for agriculture. In both cases sustainability can mean the beginning of an age of endless energy and abundant food, through conservation and the responsible use of our renewable resources. As one friend quipped, referring to the Slow Food movement, what we need as we figure out how to relocalize energy production is a Slow Fuel movement.

To be sure, entrenched political and business interests will not willingly relinquish their stranglehold on the status quo. But the dramatic rise of local and organic food production means two things: one, that the new agrarians are becoming more self-confident as they move from the margins into the mainstream; and two, that the ecological production of food, fiber, and fuel has proven itself to be just as effective as the industrial model. Technological innovation is not the problem. Nor is the natural world our nemesis. Organic farming has taught us that when it comes to creating a sustainable future, nature is actually our staunchest ally. Our greatest challenge is not figuring out how to produce more but how to share what we already have.

In California, a brilliant initiative called Roots of Change (ROC) has been launched. After being incubated by a consortium of foundations, it is now an independent effort that has the laudable goal of making California agriculture sustainable by 2030. ROC is taking the initiative on one of the thorniest issues facing the sustainable movement, the economic disparities caused by race and class. At a series of meetings held in the spring of 2007 to discuss strategy, the issues of race and privilege were openly and frankly discussed. The problem runs deep in agriculture, with its legacy of plantations and slavery. Black farmers have faced continual and systematic racial and economic discrimination, and we have a sorry history of mistreating migrant farmworkers. But the environmental and sustainable agriculture movements are tackling this issue head on and struggling to articulate a new theory of social change acceptable to all participants.

At first this was a hidden problem that no one wanted to touch. Then it became a matter of inclusion, of who's in the room. Then it was a matter of who's at the table, of who has a say in making policy. Finally, it's about core values and who decides the agenda in the first place. The tone of the current conversation can be summed up by repeating the adage attributed to a small third world community about how to help those in need. It goes like this: When well-meaning outsiders arrive bringing aid, they are told, "If you came here to help me, you can go home. But if you see that my struggle and your struggle are the same, then stay, and let us begin finding a way to work together." The Honduran leader of the worldwide peasant organization Via Campesina, Rafael Alegria, says, "What really unites us is a fundamental commitment to humanism. [It's] the antithesis of individualism and materialism. The common problems of land, production, technology, markets... these we have in common. What unites us are great aspirations." There is one thing most people involved agree on, and that is that the full potential of the sustainability movement will be realized only if it addresses both community diversity and ecological integrity.

Jim Cochran is an organic strawberry farmer in California. His farm has always been unionized, and he's worked to incorporate the needs of his farmworkers into his business. He says that instead of increasing the scale of operations, sustainable growers should increase their productivity. He means we should raise the number of producers, not the size of their operations. He is joined by many others who estimate that in order to raise the level of production of sustainable agriculture to that of industry, we will need millions of new farmers. This, of course, is an enormous economic opportunity, one that young people are taking seriously.

Leading the way are some inspiring collaborative strategies coming from some surprising places. In poverty-stricken West Oakland, People's Grocery runs an urban agriculture and enterprise development program with "Good 4 U" snack stands and a mobile van that provides access to fresh organic produce in a neighborhood where there are no grocery stores. The Watts Garden Club in Southern California, run by "the seed lady," Anna Marie Carter, works with former gang members and local youth to teach them about gardening and healthy food. Hispanic migrant workers and Asian immigrants are starting their own farms, many of them organic, and selling culturally specific foods they grow directly to their communities. In the Northwest, farming, Native American, and fishing communities are working together to save salmon habitat. "When you look at who's going into farm-ing," says author Anna Lappé, "it's young people, it's women, it's immigrants."

Native Seeds/SEARCH in the Southwest is doing extraordi-nary work saving traditional seeds and working collaboratively. It has joined with the Cultural Conservancy, a Native American land restoration group, on a project called Renewing America's Food Traditions (RAFT). Along with the Chefs Collaborative, Slow Food, and others, RAFT is bringing native farmers, con-servationists, ranchers, seed savers, and restaurants together to ensure the long-term prosperity and environmental integrity of local food cultures throughout North America. Native American studies professor Melissa Nelson, who works with RAFT, says she became interested in native food traditions because "native cultures—their languages, songs, dances, ceremonies, and ways of knowing—are all inspired by the beauty and diversity of the natural world around them as well as their daily interaction with all of it. Plants, for instance, are shaped by the hands of the native people, who depend on them for food, for medicine, and for their identity."

When the food, farming, and environmental groups find com-mon cause with the economic development and social justice movements, the combination will create an irresistible force for change. There are already emergent possibilities in these activities that are powerfully arrayed in favor of sustainability and social justice. It turns out that in all the great work being done by these new agrarians, the two themes that surface most are the impor-tance of seed saving and the urgent need to re-create local food systems. All this is bringing about the most important change of all: a resurgence of respect for the importance of indigenous plant knowledge. Even more endangered than the plants themselves is the traditional knowledge that native people have fostered through their long relationships with the plant communities they have been tending for thousands of years.

Putting the Culture Back into Agriculture

When early European explorers arrived in California, they noted in their journals that the land looked like the parks they loved at home. They assumed that the local people lived off the natural bounty of the land. What they didn't see was that these "parks" were created with the skill and expertise California Indians were using to manage the land for its optimal productivity. Instead of planting orchards, they burned underbrush that competed with native oaks to increase the production of acorns, their staple food. They harvested edible bulbs in ways that made them larger and more numerous. They tended grasses to maximize the amount of seeds they set. Instead of domesticating animals, they cleared meadows and then hunted the game that went there to graze.

According to Malcolm Margolin, publisher of Heyday Books and *News from Native California,* Indians from five different language groups along just one river divvied up the fishing rights to maximize the catch for everyone. M. Kat Anderson's book *Tending the Wild* is full of extraordinary examples of how native people used highly adaptive technologies and tools, especially fire. Left unattended, California's wildlands would have become an impenetrable thicket, fueling the kind of disastrous fires we experience today. Burning was an important native practice that kept areas clear, and many useful native plants in California were adapted to it. Margolin says, "I continue to marvel at the wonderfully elaborate knowledge that native people have about the plant world, about the timing of plant life and the use of things. When Europeans came, they dismissed native food systems and imposed a foreign system of agriculture on the land. It enabled us to live here in great numbers, but I keep wondering what was lost—a whole other mode of dealing with the plant world that is gracious, reciprocal, and mutually beneficial."

Indigenous communities everywhere developed highly complex adaptive systems for food production and cultural practices that kept their resources in productive balance for thousands of years. There are exceptions, but surviving cultures demonstrate the resilience of their strategies. There is a one-to-one correlation between cultural diversity and biological diversity. Most of the biological diversity remaining in the world is cared for by native communities that rely on their ancestral knowledge of plants and land use as well as communal property systems and oral tradition. Their spiritual life is fully integrated into the natural and social life of their communities. These are the original "plant whisperers," accomplished practitioners of the ancient art of long-term observation of and interaction with the natural world.

One place in the United States where the integration of land, community, water, seeds, and culture is still honored in daily life is northern New Mexico. The upper Rio Grande is the most culturally rich landscape in the nation, with twenty Native American nations and Hispanics, Mexicanos, Chicanos, and Anglos all living together in a sparse, high, dry desert. The *acequias* and Pueblo associations, groups that maintain the ancient water systems in the area, have declared themselves GMO-free zones and pledged to protect the traditional varieties of the crops they grow. This is where the Traditional Native American Farmers Association, the Pueblos, local farmers, and activists gathered in 2006 to work out an agreement on the most fundamental aspect of their work, what they call "seed sovereignty."

Miguel Santistevan is a handsome, thoughtful, hip young farmer with a master's degree in biology who works for the New Mexico Acequia Association. His goal is to protect all of the traditional seeds and water systems of the area. The *acequias* are a network of canals that thread through the high desert, distributing water from the mountains into fields in amounts that are sufficient for everyone's use throughout the summer. The *acequias* are a shared resource, a common good maintained by local groups through a highly sophisticated common property system. Not surprisingly, they are under assault by developers who want their water.

Part of Santistevan's work is preserving the ancient irrigation systems used by the Pueblos. Some of the native waterways predate the *acequia* system, which was brought to the area by the

Spanish. Santistevan says that the *acequia* system originated in the high desert areas of the Middle East. The Arabs took this technology to northern Africa and then the Moors took it to Spain, and from there this ingenious way of growing food in dry lands was brought to New Mexico. There, the careful arrangement of trees and crops, how the water is directed to the plants, and the yearly cleaning of the canals is worked out communally and managed by a person called a majordomo.

Santistevan works with local youth groups, tribes, community gardens, and the *acequia* associations to weave together stronger support for traditional ways of life. He does it all with a refreshing confidence and hope for the future and by combining his wide-ranging interests in permaculture, traditional farming, local economic development, and cultural preservation. His number-one goal, he says, is to get the youth to plant seeds. "It's an untrue stereotype that kids don't want to work outside. They can do the work, they are into it. I see it all the time—they love it. Work makes them feel tough and accomplished."

Santistevan tells a moving story about how he, as a young man, fell in love with corn. He was hanging out with some people who "volunteered" him to help plant corn, even though he had never planted anything before. They sent him off to get the seeds they needed, drawing a map to a remote place where an old man lived. "The place was awesome," Santistevan says. "This old guy, he had these barrels, and, well, this is where it all starts, man. He had these barrels in his carport, like a trash can, but it was full of blue corn seed. I never seen anything like that before. He told me to put my hands in it." Santistevan's voice begins to waver with strong feelings as he goes on with his story. "This old man, he told me to put my hands in. 'Feel the corn,' he says. 'Feel what's in your hands. That's your life in your hands. This is why you are alive. Now take this, go and plant it.'" Santistevan stops here, his deep emotion apparent as his eyes brim and his voice shakes. This, he says, is how he began his work.

When Santistevan talks about saving seed, he is just as expressive. Like most northern New Mexicans, he weaves English and Spanish together. He describes how he came to understand how the corn seed exchanges in the area worked. He learned that *es necesario,* it's necessary, to have corn that drinks from *un otro río,* another river. The old-timers, he says, used to say that corn that drinks the water of another river is different. "You need different corns that drink from different waters." He talks about how the local communities store and share seed and how his bolita beans, which are small, delicious, and drought-resistant, will save everyone when the water runs out.

Global warming is a big motivator, Santistevan says. "We don't want to have to stand in line or go back to how it was. We want to do it ourselves. We can do it like before the Spanish came, when the Pueblos had six years of food stored. That comes from experience with drought. That's the intergenerational memory of the landscape." It used to be, he explains, that the water, the seeds, and the land were all one. No one could conceive of selling or owning water or seeds. It's all part of the same thing, that connection between people, place, and plants, he says. "It's the reason we want to keep our seed sovereignty."

Santistevan is proud of the collaborations taking place in New Mexico, which are protecting the ways of life of traditional farmers, their water, and their seeds. They all reject the idea of genetically engineered seed, he says, laughing. "Yeah, but making a place a GMO-free zone or establishing seed sovereignty is like putting up a sign that says BURGLARY-FREE ZONE. You can only hope the burglars see the sign and respect it. It can't work, you know. The way to go has to be through education. We go find elders who have seed. We learn from them. We take the seeds and grow them out. We get kids involved in learning the knowledge and techniques. We have an in-situ seed-saving farm, producing local food security, as well as a youth development program." Santistevan speaks with a heady mix of languages and thought systems, in a way that feels enormously reassuring. Listening to him is like seeing all our dreams of social, environmental, and economic sustainability come together in one young man dedicated to working it all out for the future.

This is how Santistevan describes his approach: "You take a kid out to the field, you help them plant a seed—corn, say—and then you go back in August and harvest it, and when they taste the corn from the seed they planted, well, let me tell you, you got them for life. You got them for life. They will never go back to fast food. You take the hardest, roughest, most inattentive so-called hoodlum, and you take them out in the field, plant a seed, have them open up the ground, and you will see the transformation in them. That's what keeps my work going. That's the best part of my life, working the land and the kids."

NINE

A Conversation with Corn

Without corn, North America—and most particularly modern, technological North America—
is inconceivable.

MARGARET VISSER,
Much Depends on Dinner

Sierra Madre de Oaxaca, Mexico

This mountainous region in southern Mexico is a rich mosaic of
oak and pine forests and indigenous farming communities. It's
also the cradle of corn. Small Zapotec Indian villages lie scattered
along narrow mountain roads and in secluded valleys. Chickens
bustle and peck while small dogs sleep in sunlit town squares.
Clear water from the mountains flows through the towns, into
household gardens and public fountains, then on to the *milpas*,
where corn, beans, and squash are grown. On the outskirts of
town, larger fields are farmed collectively and the surrounding
forest is managed communally. The Zapotec have lived here for
thousands of years, and they have developed ways of governing
and sustaining themselves that maintain an intricate balance between their needs, the demands of the plants and animals they live
with, and the particularity of this land. They are the descendants
of the farmers who, living here and elsewhere in southern Mexico, first domesticated corn over 7,000 years ago.

This is also the area where, as we have seen, genetically modified corn was found among the local corn varieties in 2001. This area is part of the center of origin of corn. Centers of origin are those few places on earth where the original genetic ancestors and weedy relatives of the crops we use still survive. And centers of origin are the areas where the greatest diversity of these plants can be found. When a crop is cultivated in one area for thousands of years, people find ways to select and adapt variations in plants that respond well to different ecological niches. Eighty-five thousand specialized subvarieties of corn are known in the Oaxaca region alone, according to one local expert.

Corn has developed ways to tolerate wind, drought, crowding, and an assortment of diseases and pests. There is even a type of corn that fixes its own nitrogen. This interplay of plant, place, and people is the basis for genetic diversity in crops. Centers of origin and diversity are the world's most important living treasure chests of genetic variability. This is where the genes the world will need when its modern varieties are attacked by pests, disease, and global warming are preserved.

When GMOs arrived in Capulalpam, corn had come full circle, from its indigenous origins in Mexico to the industrial fields of the Midwest and then back home again. When Ignacio Chapela, the lead scientist who first discovered the contamination, returned to this area early in 2002, I accompanied him. I wanted to find out how transgenic corn had come to these remote mountain villages and how it might affect the lives of the people here. And I was curious to know what this story tells us about the way we grow corn in the United States, how corn came to be genetically transformed and made into a commodity, and what we can learn now from corn and indigenous corn cultures.

The complex social and farming systems that gave rise to corn are still practiced by the Zapotec in Mexico. Anthropologist Roberto Gonzalez says, for instance, that it's common for a Zapotec to say, "Maize has a heart." This has some biological truth, since a corn kernel does have a nucleus, or heart, from which the seed germinates. But the villagers use the term "heart" in the moral sense as well. They view corn as a "plant-person with a long memory, a strict moral code, and an unshakable will." Most important, to the Zapotec, corn always "prescribes reciprocity." In places where there are constant land conflicts, this reciprocity helps bind communities together and keeps the peace. Reciprocity influences market transactions, cultural traditions, and seed exchanges. "Thus maize is not only an economic good," says Gonzalez, "but a medium through which certain social and moral obligations, particularly reciprocity—toward kin, neighbors, poorer villagers, and people in neighboring villages—must be met." When a favor is done, a favor is returned.

Reciprocity is also embedded in the practice of *gozona,* a mutual aid arrangement whereby services are freely exchanged. Decisions in the community are made through a consensus process, and leadership positions are rotated. The Zapotec communities in the Sierra Norte understand that if they maintain corn, it will maintain them. This concept, referred to as *mantenimiento,* or maintenance, is crucial. By keeping their faith in corn, by planting it and caring for it, the Zapotec made sure that corn proliferated. This relationship, not men in white coats in laboratories, resulted in the development of 20,000 distinct varieties of corn.

To sustain these traditional values, the Zapotec are vigilant about their way of life. The coming of transgenic corn to these communities signaled the potential for profound cultural transformation. Without intervention, it might mean the end of these ancient traditions as well as their legacy of conserving local plant varieties. When we lose these traditions, we don't just lose the land, the plants, and the people; we lose their perspective. Our industrial relationship with corn has resulted in widespread economic and environmental ruin in just a few decades. The Zapotec's traditional relationship with corn has sustained them for thousands of years. Can we really consider our way superior?

Part of the tragedy is that this GMO contamination was entirely predictable. Corn is well known for being promiscuous in the way it spreads its pollen around. Farmers love to experiment with corn seed. Corn owes its very existence to this intentional and accidental recombination of genes. As soon as any transgenic corn was allowed into Mexico, it was only a matter of time before these foreign genes would get out and mix with the locals.

It turns out that GMO corn found its way to these remote mountains courtesy of NAFTA, the North American Free Trade Agreement. Free trade agreements force Mexico to import millions of tons of corn each year. Since most of it comes from the United States, most of it is highly contaminated with GMOs. This imported corn is then distributed throughout Mexico by the government to the government-run Diconsa stores. But there are no labels on the corn, no warnings to farmers not to plant the seed. The free trade rules were not written for Mexican farmers; they were created for the benefit of grain traders, who do not want labels used.

Señora Olga Toro Maldonado is a farmer from the village of Capulalpam. Her fields were contaminated with GMOs. She said she was distressed to find out that those fat kernels of corn for sale in her village store contained GMOs. How, she asked, was she supposed to know they shouldn't be planted? Now her seed was unusable and she was worried about feeding her six children. The situation was grave, for her and others in the village. The mayor of Capulalpam, Javier Cosmes Perez, said, "Our customs are being violated." GMOs "upset us because it has to do with our traditions, the essence of our people, and our lives, our corn."

Under NAFTA, corn grown in the United States by farmers who are subsidized is sent to Mexico. This cheap corn then competes with local corn grown by farmers who are not subsidized. In 2002, corn in the Diconsa store was selling for four or five pesos a kilogram. Local farmers said it cost them six to seven pesos a kilogram to grow their local varieties, and many of them said they could no longer afford to farm. This is evident in eerily empty small towns all across the Sierra Norte. Older men, women, and children live there, but many of the adult men support their families by going north to find jobs in *maquiladora* factories on the border or by doing farmwork in the very places in the United States that grow the corn that put them off their land.

Americans feel the impact too, as we struggle to cope with

the massive migration caused by the impoverishment of rural Mexico, Guatemala, and other Central American countries. Supporting these rural economies would not only keep their village families intact, it would ensure the preservation of crop genetic diversity. Mexico's 3 million farmers feed themselves and provide food for 15 million other poor rural people. They sustain their local economies while conserving critical local varieties of corn and other native food crops, such as squash and peppers. They also preserve their own diverse farming traditions and guarantee the continuation of their country's rich plant genetic diversity. All of those benefits to biodiversity are threatened by the economics of the global grain trade.

After the GMO contamination in the Sierra Norte was discovered, the Mexican government and other organizations did their own surveys. They too found widespread GMO contamination of corn, confirming the earlier results. Then, in 2003 and 2004, further sampling found no spread of the contamination. One participant in the later studies suggested that farmers had been careful not to plant imported corn and by doing so had apparently eliminated the contamination. Dr. Chapela reviewed their results and said that the later studies based their conclusions on the presence of "negligible" transgenes. Essentially, Chapela says, the GMOs were there, they just got lost in translation. By interpreting the findings differently, they concluded that GMOs were no longer present. Plus, Chapela says, some of their results matched his findings. Another widespread study of the effects of transgenic corn in Mexico was done in 2004, under the questionable patronage of NAFTA. It covered all the bases and was generally vague in its conclusions. Nevertheless, the threat of contamination remains as long as Mexico allows GMO corn inside its borders and fails to protect its rich indigenous farming traditions.

Major Goodman says that several problems threaten the diversity and integrity of corn in Mexico, not just GMOs. He told me that the threat which concerns him most is the increasing use of hybrid corn varieties there, which, in his opinion, will affect Mexico's genetic resources as much as transgenics. A 2006 study conducted by CIMMYT, the international CGIAR corn and wheat seed bank in Mexico, echoes this concern. It concluded that because of government efforts to promote "modern" agriculture, specialized and local varieties of corn in the southeastern state of Chiapas have already been replaced by improved varieties and hybrids. CIMMYT said that "maize landraces have virtually disappeared" in one region of Chiapas. (Landraces are genetically variable populations of a crop that respond differently to local conditions.) In 2000, 90 percent of the area was sown to open-pollinated maize varieties and landraces. Now 90 percent of the area is in hybrids, and only 5 percent is planted with landraces and 5 percent with other open-pollinated varieties.

The most important thing the study reported was that "the traditional practice of exchanging seed has almost disappeared." The study area is the mountainous home of the Zapatista uprising and a gateway for undocumented immigrants from Central America, still plagued by poverty. Local people prefer the landraces for making tortillas and other food, but they are low-yield. As the report details, when farmers switched to improved, hybrid maize, they were given seed, fertilizer, and pesticides as well as technical advice and crop loss insurance, all on credit, to be repaid at harvest. The problem is that these improved hybrids pay off only when they are supported with these expensive inputs and grown in a good year. The report noted that "when you have a bad year, like recent ones with hurricanes or droughts, the investment in seed and other inputs exposes farmers to potential losses many cannot afford." This is the same model used to push improved seeds on rural communities throughout the Southern Hemisphere, and it is impoverishing them as they get locked in a cycle of debt.

The Double Cross

A deeper understanding of the story of corn involves weaving together bits of archaeology, anthropology, botany, agronomy, economic history, and mythology. Corn arrived in the United States nearly 4,000 years ago. Tiny ears of corn that old have been found in New Mexico in an area previously thought to be inhabited only by simple prehistoric hunting communities. We now know that 2,000 years before the time of Christ, the beautiful desert landscape of the Southwest was supporting a rich, complex system of agricultural communities. Vast residential complexes were constructed in Chaco Canyon, with five-story buildings, massive circular underground *kivas,* and structures that had eight hundred rooms, all built five hundred years before Europeans reached our shores. According to legend, Chaco was built by "the people of the seed," corn clans with direct ancestral links to native peoples still living in the area today.

Corn's extraordinary capacity to adapt to varied conditions means that it can grow almost anywhere. Where it's grown well, people do well. After thriving in Mexico for a few thousand years, corn spread to southern Canada and South America. According to Charles Mann, there were between 90 and 112 million people living in the Western Hemisphere in 1491, the year before Columbus arrived. That means the Americas supported a population larger than Europe's.

In Mexico, agriculture was already established at least 10,000 years ago, as evidenced by domesticated squash seeds found there. New discoveries continually push back the date for early farming all over the Americas. Likewise, the sophisticated civilizations of the Maya, Inca, and Aztecs discredit any outdated notions about the superiority of the invading Western civilization. Civilizations in Central and South America supported robust and healthy populations; their cities had wide, clean boulevards, hanging gardens, and vast temple complexes. The people practiced highly developed medicine and shamanism, had long-distance communication and trade, and had an understanding of astronomy and mathematics that surpassed anything known in Europe at the time.

It has been said that the "invention" of corn is one of the great achievements of all time. It ranks right up there with the use of fire and the wheel. Walton Galinat, author of *Maize: Gift from America's First Peoples,* said that Columbus failed to recognize that corn was far more valuable than the gold he sought and that "this plant, developed by peoples he judged poor and uncivilized, far outstripped in productivity any of the cereals bred by Old World farmers—wheat, rice, sorghum, barley, and rye."

By the time Columbus arrived, North America was already a corn-fed continent. Early farmers saw the value of the natives' open-pollinated seeds and copied their practices. According to Mann, the Indians worked on such a grand scale that it was hard for Europeans to imagine. Rather than domesticating animals for meat, they managed large ecosystems, using nature to maintain huge populations of plants and animals. In 1491, North America was a vast, highly productive, and well-managed landscape. But gradually Europeans imposed their values on the land "by breaking it into fragments for farmers and herders." The European practice of supporting isolated populations of plants and animals, who were taken out of their natural context and "domesticated," or made dependent on people, meant that they had to go to great lengths to rearrange the landscape. Cutting trees, fencing, and diverting rivers for food production were just the beginning. For a time, the natural bounty of the native soil provided these newcomers with years of productivity. But immigrant practices that relied on extraction rather than reciprocity soon mined out the generosity of the land.

Farming continued as a community endeavor, and seed saving and exchange were a vital part of the local economy well into the twentieth century. An endearing story about the farmer who grew prizewinning corn captures the original spirit of rural America. Every year he took his best ears of corn to the state fair, where they won first prize. One year a reporter asked the farmer how he grew such great corn. The farmer said that he always made sure that he shared his best corn seed with his neighbors. "How can you afford to share your best seed with your neighbors when they are entering the same corn competition as you each year?" the reporter asked. "Why, sir," said the farmer, "don't you know? The wind picks up the pollen from the ripening corn and swirls it from field to field. If my neighbors grow inferior corn, cross-pollination will steadily degrade the quality of my corn. If I am to grow good corn, I must help my neighbors grow good corn."

Farming in America was not fully industrialized until after World War II. But the foundation for that transformation was laid in the 1920s and '30s with the creation of hybrid corn seed. Getting farmers to switch from open-pollinated corn, which they could regenerate themselves, to hybrids, which they had to buy, took a lot of persuasion and spawned new promotional techniques, which we now know as focus groups and viral marketing. When the New Deal electrified the farm, radio advertising began to change farmers' expectations about what they could accomplish by themselves. Farmers began to be less self-reliant and more willing to become dependent on commercial help to solve their problems. The radical transformation of agriculture was accomplished by the three-step process of first selling farmers hybrid seed, then switching them to GMOs, and finally ending their capacity and right to save seed altogether.

Hybridization has long been observed and understood, but the hybrid corn planted all across America now is a sophisticated modern version, a double cross of two inbred lines. Early in the twentieth century, breeders experimented with the single cross of corn and realized some "hybrid vigor." It didn't produce well enough to compete with open-pollinated seed. Corn breeding, public and private, was stymied until the double-cross hybrid was created and became cost-competitive. Corn growing was forever changed.

The success of hybrid corn has been attributed to the business acumen, and no small sense of showmanship, of one remarkable man, Henry A. Wallace. Wallace served as secretary of agriculture and then vice president under President Franklin D. Roosevelt. He was the son of Henry C. Wallace, the secretary of agriculture for President Warren Harding. And he founded the Hi-Bred Corn Company, a leader in early hybrid corn research, which later became Pioneer Hi-Bred International. Wallace used contests, corn shows, and state fairs to popularize hybrid corn. He worked tirelessly to get farmers to adopt hybrids, and his position in both the public and the private sectors makes him unique. He was proud of his accomplishments, once boasting that "we hear a great deal about atomic energy. Yet I am convinced that historians will rank the harnessing of hybrid [corn] power as equally significant."

Some might say that hybrid corn became the atom bomb of agriculture. As with all technologies, its development is a combination of the invention itself and the intentions with which it is developed and deployed. In 1982, Harvard geneticist Richard Lewontin remarked, "Since the 1930s, immense effort has been put into getting better and better hybrids. Virtually no one has tried to improve the open-pollinated varieties, although scientific evidence shows that if the same effort had been put into such varieties, they would be as good or better than hybrids by now." Hybrid corn revolutionized American agriculture, but it had a devastating impact on the American family farm, because it took away farmers' independence. In a sense it's the great double-cross of American agriculture, because it turned the farmer from a producer into a consumer.

The Decline and Fall of the Corn Empire

Willard Cochrane, agricultural adviser to President John F. Kennedy, said that in the end, he felt the increasing reliance of agriculture on private corporations was catastrophic for American farmers. He said, "For the vast majority of farmers, the agricultural development process based on rapid and widespread technological advance has been a nightmare." As farmers spiraled down into dependence, they were pushed to overproduce. That kept prices down, far below the costs of production. Until the ethanol boom, corn farmers were getting two dollars for a bushel of corn that cost them three dollars to grow. Carl Sandburg described the corn empire best in his poem *Good Morning, Amer-*

ica, written in 1928: "We raise more corn to feed more hogs, to buy more land, to raise more corn to feed more hogs..."

Feeding hogs is what the 80 million acres of corn grown in the United States every year is all about. Almost all of that corn is field corn, grown for animal feed and industrial uses. Corn is used to make adhesives, plastics, medicines, and sweeteners. The overproduction of corn has led to some of our most serious diet-related health problems, such as the overuse of high-fructose corn syrup in soft drinks and other snacks that cause obesity. The fat in corn-fed cattle clogs our arteries. Corn was not meant for cows, either. They are designed to eat grass. Corn-fed cattle are more vulnerable to disease than cattle fed diets more suitable to their digestive systems. Corn-fed cattle consume (and excrete) vast quantities of antibiotics. The beef, milk, and corn products in supermarkets come laced with the long-lasting herbicide Atrazine, a toxic chemical widely used in America but banned in many European countries.

The monocropping of corn is an environmental problem in its own right. It contributes to soil loss, the reduction of biological diversity, and the widespread use of chemical pesticides and fertilizers that pollute the water and our food. Almost half of this industrial corn crop is genetically modified. The insecticide inside many of these plants is having its own environmental impact on beneficial insects and other unintended targets, including the monarch butterfly. These engineered corn plants are an artificial mimic of the real thing. Now we can use corn to drive our machines as well as our metabolisms.

How long can we feast on the persistent illusion that we can get along without nature after all? Is there no intelligence other than our own? I ask these questions because it seems to me that we, as children of corn, have much to learn from corn, and we could take some farming lessons and lessons on how to maintain community life from the patrons of corn, the Zapotec. Corn is an amazing life form. It has a miraculous ability to capture sunlight and turn it into food, fiber, and fuel. This giant green photosynthetic miracle is actually the result of corn's eagerness to please us and its willingness to adapt to the places where we ask it to grow. Corn has a lot to teach us about interdependence, flexibility, and adaptation, if we'd only care to learn.

Listening to Corn

Corn is one of the great communicators of the plant world. Corn listens, too. It constantly monitors its environment, checking how close other plants are, sensing moisture, temperature, and light. Corn contacts the funguses, bacteria, insects, worms, and other microorganisms in the soil to see how they're doing. Then it recruits them into its own growth strategy. Corn can even send out an alarm when its leaves are injured. An astounding study published in *Nature* found that when a caterpillar munches on corn leaves, the plant emits a chemical that attracts a tiny wasp which flies over and stings the caterpillar and then lays its eggs in its tissues. The wasp's reward is a home for its eggs, and the corn is protected. And by the way, corn has more genes than humans do, if numbers count for anything.

Although corn may be one of the best-known plants in the world, we're still unraveling its mysteries. We know corn is a giant tropical grass that in most of the world is called maize. Its botanical name is *Zea mays*. It grows exceedingly fast, sometimes more than 4 inches a day. Midwestern farmers claim to be able to hear their corn growing. It is a sound poetically described by Margaret Visser as the "gentle stroke and rasp of leaves unfurling and sweeping along stalk and leaf edge: the hum of the driving wheel of North American civilization." Still, the botanical origins of corn remain lost in the mists of time and myth. Some of the world's preeminent botanists have spent their entire careers searching for its wild ancestors, without success. Corn's closest known relatives are two wild Mexican grasses, *teosinte* and *Tripsacum*. Combining them does not produce corn as we know it. The one that is closest, *teosinte*, is still four chromosomes off. So no single mutation or recombination of the known wild grasses can account for what we know as corn.

The fact that we do not know the botanical ancestor of corn makes it unique in the world of food plants. But corn is unusual for another reason. It could not exist without people. Because of the way kernels cling to the cob and the way the cob is tightly wrapped in a sheath of fibrous leaves, someone or something has to strip off the seeds and disperse them. Corn asks those who use it to assist in its propagation. It's an arrangement that has worked well for all concerned.

Where might we have gone wrong? According to an early admonition from a Native American story, our decline as a culture began when we started feeding corn to animals instead of primarily to ourselves. I might suggest that it was ensured when we began thinking of corn as a machine, and then, as a result, we began treating it as a machine. Now we use it to feed our machines. This is not just a metaphor. Genetically engineered corn can be patented because our society regards engineered genes as a mechanistic invention. Wendell Berry has written that the idea of living things as machines may have begun as metaphor, but it has evolved "from metaphor through equation to identification." We can see how this plays out. Corn, once the goddess of pre-Columbian Mexico, the source of fertility and life, has now been engineered by one California company to produce human contraceptives. This, to me, is an abject failure of the human imagination. And from the plant's point of view, it's a dead end.

The botanical ancestry of corn may not be known, but its mythological origins are rich, and they suggest a way out of this maze (pardon the pun). Many corn creation stories are strikingly similar. One repeated theme is the idea that corn was given to humans as a gift. It usually comes from some divine source, often mediated by an animal or insect. Corn was frequently given to humans in response to a plea for help or as a way to stave off hunger. Sometimes a sacrifice was required. Invariably, along with the gift of corn there came a set of instructions about the responsibilities that humans had toward it. These ancient teachings caution us to maintain a respectful reciprocity with corn in order to ensure that its gifts will be continually replenished.

This relationship worked for thousands of years. Corn formed the cultural and economic foundations of the ancient cultures of the Americas. Murals and stone carvings in Mexico and Guatemala depict Aztec and Mayan corn and the people's gods and goddesses as inseparable. Corn is shown growing from the deities' heads and being given blood sacrifices. Corn, as the lord of maize, is shown as the tree of life. Corn is shown growing as the hair of the corn goddess, and corn plants sprout heads of people with faces shaped as cobs. Corn continues to be central to native cultures in the American Southwest—the Hopi, Pueblos, and Navajos—and to Hispanic farming communities.

Corn is still grown in traditional ways in the forest gardens of the Mandan, the Hidatsa, the Mohawk, and the Ojibwa, and it's revered in the green corn ceremony of the traditional Seminole in Florida. The common thread throughout these communities is that corn is sacred. It's regarded as a regenerative life-giving force, constantly reconnecting people to their land and community as well as the cycles of life, death, and rebirth.

The Hopi creation story helps explain their worldview and tells us something about ourselves and our modern attitude toward corn. The version of the story I use is based on Frank Waters's classic work, *The Book of the Hopi.* Since the beginning of their existence, the Hopi have emerged through several different worlds. Whenever they were overwhelmed by wickedness or corruption, their world would be destroyed and they went underground. Later they reemerged into the next world. And at each emergence, the Creator gave them corn for sustenance.

By the time of the Fourth World, the one we are living in now, there were many people who had already divided into races. The Creator decided to find out how much greed and ignorance there was among the humans. Many ears of corn were laid out. They were all different shapes, sizes, and colors. The people were told, "The time has come for you to make an Emergence to a new world. There you will spread out, multiply, and populate the earth. So choose now, according to your wisdom, the corn you will take with you to be your food." People came forward and took different ears—long ears, fat ears, and big ears of different colors. Only one people, the Hopi, held back and waited. All that was left was the smallest ear. They said this ear was like "the original humble ear given them on the First World, and they knew it would never die out." They knew this corn could grow without water and would help them survive in the harsh climate where they lived.

The Hopi have survived in the high Arizona desert for thousands of years. Their corn beliefs are integral to that success. The key phrase in the instruction is to choose "according to your wisdom." The continuity of the Hopi culture is living testimony to the wisdom of the long-standing symbiotic relationship between themselves, their homelands, and the corn that is the sacred center of their lives. They exemplify the enduring value of the bond between plants, people, and place. Waters says that these three elements are so synonymous for the Hopi "that it is difficult to tell which was created first, land, man, or corn."

This indigenous view of corn is obviously in sharp contrast to our own culture's view, which has produced the vast "corndom" of the Midwest. From what I can tell, this must be where all the big fat yellow ears of corn in the Hopi story went to live. It's the land of the singing plow and the fuming tractor and now the GPS-guided combine—the machines that transformed the magnificent grasslands of the prairie into a land of excess. Corn may be the economic machine that drives American agriculture, but if that's all we ask of corn, we diminish corn, and ourselves. Would it be possible for an ordinary person to develop a respectful relationship with corn? And if so, where do we start? As inhabitants of North America, I suggest we look to our own corn cultures for some corn wisdom.

The people of the Santo Domingo pueblo in New Mexico maintain their traditional lifestyle. The pueblo is closed to the public and has no casino. Its large, dry, dirt plaza is surrounded with mud-brick houses. Once a year they invite everyone to come visit and to participate in their corn dance. All traditional corn cultures have songs about the planting, harvesting, grinding,

and ceremonial uses of corn. What's remarkable about one particular song of the Santo Domingo tradition is that it is not sung
by the people, it's sung by the corn.

The song, as recorded and transcribed in the 1930s, is being
reprinted here in part with permission of the Santo Domingo
Pueblo. When the corn hears people approaching at the beginning of the harvest, it says, *Here they come now on the road with
cornmeal and prayer stick... They talk nicely to us. Then we say,
"Now is the time to go." We agree in the kindest thoughts. Of
course, then we explain to the rest of the corn, touching one another and rustling...* The song goes on to say, *How lovingly he
takes me and puts me down where I shall rest awhile.*

To me, this song, which is even more beautiful in its entirety,
demonstrates the difference between our own modern view of
corn and the traditional one. The Pueblo's song gracefully ac-
knowledges corn's feelings and recognizes the propriety with
which it expects to be treated. It is a poetic expression of the
essence of love, which is the ability to see the world through the
eyes of the beloved.

Corn remains a powerful part of the spirit of our country. It
continues to provide generously for many of our basic needs. In
1963, Frank Waters asked, "Have we of the Synthetic Age grown
so far away from the earth that we read no meaning in the elements of its minerals, plant, and animal kingdoms?" He's suggesting that our survival depends as much on our ability to derive
meaning from the natural world as on any means we develop to
exploit it. This is the lesson of corn. If the miracles of corn are to
continue, we will need to find a place for corn, not just in our
fields and on our dinner tables but in our hearts as well.

TEN

The Down-Turned Hand

> Somewhere between the resilience of communities
> that have survived through it all, the seeds and the
> people recover, and biodiversity returns despite the
> monoculture of colonialism.
>
> WINONA LADUKE, *Recovering the Sacred*

Kaua'i, Hawai'i

Wind and waves gather force over thousands of miles of open ocean, then slam into the north side of the island of Kaua'i. Razor-sharp cliffs slice down the sides of the Na Pali coast, carved from above by water falling down the mountainsides and excavated from below by winds careening up from the sea. Gashes of blood-red soil show through the soft green velour covering the land. The churning air and water form heavy clouds that dump over 440 inches of rain on Mount Wai'ale'ale every year, making it the wettest place on earth. These waters stream down the mountainsides in waterfalls and rivers and, before returning to the sea, pulse through the veins of an unbelievable diversity of plants, birds, animals, insects, and fish that live here. Viewed from above, Kaua'i looks like a large flower floating in an immense turquoise sea.

Kaua'i rose out of the Pacific Ocean 6 million years ago as part of a series of volcanic eruptions that formed the Hawaiian archipelago. When Captain Cook accidentally found these islands in

1778, Hawaiians were living self-sufficient and prosperous lives in a highly stratified society. Their religious practices derived meaning from the life of the land, the stars, and the sea. Their system of governance maximized this reciprocity with the natural world and ensured its productivity. The traditional Hawaiian diet was a healthy mix of starch and leafy greens from taro, supplemented by sweet potatoes, breadfruit, fish, fowl, and fruit and supported by a wide variety of medicinal plants. Today, however, people living in Hawai'i import over 85 percent of their food, and the descendants of the original population suffer some of the worst poverty and diet-related health problems of anyone living in the United States.

Hawai'i has everything it needs to feed itself: fertile soil, abundant water, mild climate, and skilled labor. Can it return to an economy based on local self-sufficiency? It's a question that Hawai'i is facing now and the rest of us will be facing sooner or later. As the cost of oil continues to rise, it will drive up the price of food produced by fossil fuel, especially imported foods. Local food production is the only sustainable option for the future. When it dawns on us that we're all living on what David Brower called "Earth Island," one small planet floating in the sea of space, we'll see that rising demands and declining resources are leading to a showdown. To build sustainable communities, we will have to figure out new ways to use what we already have. The greater challenge will be determining how these limited resources should be allocated, for whose benefit, and who gets to participate in these crucial decisions.

As Hawai'i begins grappling with these questions, it's worth watching. Hawai'i is farther away from another landmass than any other place on earth. It will face the energy crunch sooner than the rest of us. More important, the particular demographics of Hawai'i require it to deal with issues of race and the legacy of colonialism. The environmental movement knows that restoring integrity and diversity to the biological world means ensuring the integrity and diversity of our cultural communities.

The twentieth-century sustainability movement has proven

that we can grow healthy food in ecologically sound ways and produce sufficient energy using alternative and renewable sources. Now it's a matter of scaling up these ecological and economic achievements. What is weak is the third link in the chain, the social challenge. This third technology is what author Bill McKibben calls the "technology of community." It is essential that our solutions be place-based. The issue of place is often neglected in the search for sustainability. Placeless solutions become too focused on the technology and not enough on locality. Place is essential to the sustainability equation because our solutions have to be locally adapted and locally accepted. I have grounded each chapter in this book in a particular place as a way of emphasizing the importance of this issue.

When catastrophe hits—when the grocery store shelves and gas pumps are empty—all we'll have is each other. Communities that have already figured out how to get along with each other and how to share limited resources will be better off, not just in terms of survival but in terms of preserving local autonomy and democracy. There are agencies of government standing ready to impose authoritarian forms of control where disaster hits. They will come prepared for social unrest. Their plans assume that people will be frightened, confused, and completely dependent on outside aid for help. The Department of Homeland Security's model for disaster relief was on display for all the world to see after Hurricane Katrina hit New Orleans. But that kind of assistance will not be needed by communities that have already created the mechanisms of tolerance and local self-reliance.

Kaua'i is a small island, and yet it has an array of alternatives for the future already on display. If a road went around the entire island, you could make the drive in a few hours. Starting on the dry west side, at one end of the Na Pali coast, the existing road begins at the U.S. military's Pacific Missile Range and testing grounds. Then it continues past miles of GMO seed production and testing grounds before skirting the remains of rusting sugar mills. Then it turns toward the tourist resorts and condominiums of Po'ipu Beach. In less than an hour, you could tour all three mainstays of the current Hawaiian economy: the military, plantation agriculture, and tourism.

On the south side of the island, the road leads into the town of Lihue, where the airport, harbor, and shopping centers keep the import economy humming. Then it turns north along the ocean. Farther along the small towns thin out and a few farms and Native Hawaiian homesteads appear. Once the road passes the golf courses and resort community of Princeville, it dips down into dense jungle foliage and delivers you into another world. After crossing a one-lane bridge over a wide river, you enter Hanalei Valley, spectacularly planted with chartreuse and emerald-green taro patches. This is the North Shore, a place blessed with heartbreaking beauty and a vibrant, if somewhat fractured, local culture. The pace of life here winds down, and the road ends in the sands of Ke'e Beach, on the other side of the impassable Na Pali coast.

The North Shore is a microcosm of possibility. The people here make up a racially and economically diverse community that is beginning to create a local food economy. When the weekly farmers' market opens, the narrow road is choked with cars, bicycles, and pedestrians. Stacy Sproat-Beck, director of the Waipa Foundation, which hosts the market and grows organic food as part of its work of restoring Native Hawaiian foodways, says Waipa has counted six hundred people coming into the small outdoor market in two hours. The last time I was there, I had to jostle through a crowd and barely lost out on some Hayden mangoes to actor Pierce Brosnan, who apparently used all the charm and skills of a 007 agent to get the last ones. As the North Shore and other communities across the country are finding out, local organic food and farmers' markets are an ideal way to begin the process of bringing people together and reconnecting to each other and the places where we live.

The question for Kaua'i, as it will be for all of us, is how to choose the right model for the future. The west side of the island is living under the military-industrial model. The south side supports a kaleidoscopic array of lifestyles, with some local food production and most people shopping at big-box stores. On the north side there is an emerging model for local self-sufficiency. Most of the country has this mix of the means needed for local food and fuel production and a choice of models. But very few places have the needed leadership and proven ways to go about creating our ideal of diverse and locally controlled economies. Or at least we may not know about the rich cultural resources that are already available right where we live. In my own search for inspiration for Kaua'i, I didn't have to go very far.

Just up the road from the Waipa farmers' market, in Ha'ena, is Limahuli Garden and Preserve, part of the National Tropical Botanical Garden. Like the Waipa Foundation, the garden is engaged in an effort to restore a traditional land-use system unique to Hawai'i called an *ahupua'a* (pronounced ah-who-pooh-*ah*-ah). The *ahupua'a* is generally known as a land division, but it's better understood as a sophisticated system of sustainable resource management, an ingenious design that provided all inhabitants with access to all available resources. Most *ahupua'a* included a part of the mountain forests, freshwater streams, planting areas on the plains, fish ponds for aquaculture, and ocean reefs.

Traditionally, everyone had use rights to whatever they needed. The *ahupua'a* was managed by a *konohiki*, whose job it was to ensure that all resources were managed sustainably. This was done partly by enforcing the *kapu* system, which put various resources off-limits from time to time in order to keep them productive. The common people were required to support the *ali'i* (chiefs), but unlike European serfs, Hawaiians were not bound to a certain place. They were free to move if they didn't like the way they were treated. That meant that the *konohiki* was motivated to keep them happy. Everyone's welfare depended on the functioning of the whole, and the distribution of resources functioned as common property regime.

Very few *ahupua'a* remain in Hawai'i, and none support a local community in the traditional way. They were eradicated when native Hawaiian property values were replaced with private property rights. The natural resources of the islands were plundered by the sandalwood trade, then by whaling, and then by sugar and cattle. Massive tracts of land and traditional water systems were converted to plantation agriculture. Native lands were summarily seized and redistributed. The monarchy was overthrown, and a constitution that was written by and for American interests was imposed on the islands. And yet despite the ravages of colonialism and its modern cousins tourism and consumerism, some memory of the old ways remains. The land itself remembers. Thousands of small taro plots and water channels await the opportunity to be replanted.

Kawika Winter, a knowledgeable and engaging young Hawaiian ethnobotanist, is the director of Limahuli Garden and Preserve. He has an easy laugh and a straightforward way of explaining the complex challenges he faces in returning the land to traditional use. What people see here now, he says, is actually a collection of ideas about agriculture and landscapes that have been imposed by newcomers. This is a "*dis*integrated" place. Very few people adopt local ways, says Winter, acknowledging the difficulties of learning the complex mental, spiritual, and physical skills involved in traditional Hawaiian practices.

While I was walking around the garden, I noticed that each plant on display was marked with its botanical and common names as well as information about whether it was a native or a modern introduction. That's typical of most botanical gardens. But each native plant here also had a traditional story that was told in the garden's literature. The idea of story, of course, is central to traditional land-based cultures and their relationship to plants. The work of this garden and preserve is to save both the plants and their stories. It is a reminder that one reason we have lost so many plants, languages, places, and cultures is that we have forgotten their stories.

Severing and Remembering

The reason traditional cultures are so important to the world right now is that they still know how to remember. So much of what native people and their oral traditions are about is the simple act of remembering. It may be remembering an ancient ceremony, reenacting a dance, reciting a prayer, or reconnecting to the past through the recitation of genealogies, and, of course, through storytelling. This kind of remembering is an essential part of ecological restoration. Watershed biologist Brock Dolman says that the word "restoration" should be pronounced "re-story-ation," because it really means to "re-story" something. Many traditional people say that all restoration work begins with prayer. It begins in our hearts, because that's where the stories are kept; then we must rethink the story before we begin the work of planning restoration. Even in an age when commercial media seem to have taken over storytelling in our lives, this age-old art survives as one of the most important tools of social transformation that we have, and it is the key to achieving sustainability as well. Stories can mend our broken world.

Reestablishing communities, both social and biological, begins with the simple act of telling the stories of the inhabitants. Storytelling is remembering. To re-member is to put back together. Remembering means bringing something back to mind rather than letting it be forgotten. If we want to save places, peoples, or plants, we have to remember their stories. In their stories are the details of their natural and social history and, most important, the meaning they have for our lives. We have just about engineered the world to the point of extinction because we fail to understand what things mean and see how they are connected. That blindness is caused by forgetting. And the remedy is remembering. As writer Milan Kundera has said, "The struggle of man against power is the struggle of memory against forgetting."

The opposite of remembering is severing. To sever is to cut off. The act of severing that is most disturbing to the integrity of life on earth is the cutting of DNA. This is what genetic engineering does. It cuts into life at the molecular level. It severs something from its ancestors and changes its story. When DNA is taken from one organism and inserted into another, that new organism has a new evolutionary path, a new story, one created for it by human beings. Some people think that we have the right to control the evolution and reproduction of other organisms and that there's nothing wrong with a technology that severs our relationships to nature and our past. I believe that the use of genetic technologies to re-create the world is the defining moral issue of our time. This technology, more than any that came before it, redefines who we are, what makes us human, and how we see ourselves in relation to the rest of the natural world.

Now we are faced with a choice. Do we accept the triumph of the techno-elites, meaning do we let them decide what's best for us, or do we use our common sense and moral compass to restore the public role of humanity in evaluating and governing technology? To do the latter, we need to understand our place in the larger world and in the communities where we live. And for that we need myth and story, because they help us remember who we are and affirm our reverence for life and for the human condition. The one thing native people consistently say is that our survival depends on returning to a sense of the sacred. That means acting with respect—toward each other and the natural world. And the one thing traditional native people consistently do is engage in acts of remembering the sacred.

Some of the most effective and dynamic opposition to genetic engineering is coming from native communities. They are very clear about their responsibility to remember their stories. Many native groups strongly believe that severing DNA is an immoral act. In January 2005, a delegation of Maori scientists opposed to GMOs joined with Native American scientists and lawyers, Native Hawaiians, farmers, and activists and toured the Hawaiian Islands, literally drumming up resistance to genetic engineering through song and storytelling. The stories they told were chilling. They told of plants and animals precious to their cultures that had been taken from them. They all represented nations that had experienced the loss of their lands, their plants, their traditional knowledge, and their religious beliefs. They understood that the destruction of language and story is an essential tool of colonization, and that resistance demands acts of remembrance.

Colonization is a forced forgetting. Native communities are

responding by restoring their languages, engaging in storytelling, and reasserting their sovereignty, both political sovereignty and the sovereignty of the seed. Native groups in the United States, such as the Hopi, and in other countries, such as in India, have started seed exchanges and conferences where they "talk story," as the Hawaiians say, as a new strategy to end biotechnology and biocolonialism. The way this is playing out in Hawai'i is a good example of how both the problem and the solution are taking place at the local level.

Even though plant biotechnology has not proved itself, the research has not stopped. Plant breeders are scouring the world, looking for plants they can engineer and patent, hoping to cash in on the next genetic gold rush. Throughout history, plant collecting has always gone hand in hand with colonialism. Upright Christian explorers from Europe assumed they had the right to go anywhere in the world they wanted and to help themselves to whatever was there, wiping out native cultures along the way. This used to be justified by saying that the plants they took were needed for their own economic development or for the pursuit of knowledge. Now it's pretty much the same thing: biotechnology companies say they need to "discover" useful medicines, foods, and fuels. It's never been much more than a thinly disguised pursuit of wealth. There is a growing sense among some researchers that this "bio-piracy" is wrong. They have begun programs that provide for benefit sharing with native people when they expropriate traditional plants and plant knowledge. However, these programs still don't give indigenous people or traditional farmers any real choice in the matter, or the right to refuse entry or expropriation.

Examples of bio-piracy are legion. The latest version is the patenting of traditional crops and medicinal plants. Patents have been taken out on basmati rice, the perfumed staple rice of Pakistan and India; on a soft-milling wheat derived from a traditional variety as well as all flour, dough, and any edible products produced by it; on the neem tree, a traditional medicinal plant commonly used in India; on Native American wild rice; on plants and seeds held in public collections; and of course on every commercial variety of wheat, rice, corn, soy, and any other useful plant, fruit, and vegetable known to man, as well as on microorganisms and even nanoscale versions of 466 traditional Chinese medicines. Some of these patents have been successfully challenged, but the practice continues unabated.

The University of Hawai'i is typical of many state institutions that consider the natural resources of their state fair game. As a state agency, the university can go on state land and take any plants it wants and genetically modify or patent them without consulting the traditional users of those resources. It even entered into a bio-prospecting agreement with the Diversa Corporation, providing raw materials from state lands for Diversa to use for its commercial research and product development. In a stellar act of resistance, Native Hawaiians chained the doors of a building on campus shut as a protest over the patents the university had taken out on three traditional varieties of taro. As a result of the work of Native Hawaiians, along with the statewide anti-GMO movement and local taro farmers, a rare victory was achieved. The University of Hawai'i publicly tore up its patents on Hawaiian taro.

Walter Ritte, a Hawaiian who works with youth and teaches traditional farming on the island of Molokai'i, led the protest. He called the genetic engineering and patenting of taro a *"mana Mahele,"* referring to the Great Mahale, the historical act that broke up Hawaiian lands. He is saying that these acts destroy the *mana,* or spirit and power, of the taro. Mililani Trask, another long-time leader in the Native Hawaiian community, says GMOs threaten both the life of the land and the basic principles of Hawaiian culture. Taro is sacred to Hawaiians, she says; it is part of their ancestry, just as corn is for Native Americans. Trask says that what genetic engineers are doing to corn and what they are doing to taro, they will soon be doing to all of us. Taro and corn both have long been dependent on people to help them reproduce and have deep cultural roots in society. Taro can propagate itself by seed, but because for thousands of years people have used other plant parts, such as cut stalks, to replant it, it is losing its capacity to reproduce by seed.

To understand the importance of taro to the Hawaiian people, it helps to know even a little of its story. Taro, or *kalo* in Hawaiian, has always been far more than a source of food. In the Hawaiian creation story, the procreators of the world had a firstborn son who did not live. They buried the child. The first *kalo* plant grew from the place where the baby was buried. Their second child was the first human being and the ancestor of the Hawaiian people. Thus *kalo* is the elder brother of the Hawaiian people, someone who has always fed them. All the names for the parts of the *kalo* plant reflect this familial relationship. And the growing of *kalo* is an act of reverence for both the land and a person's genealogy.

In the 1970s, Hawaiian culture began a period of renewal. Along with it came a renaissance of traditional food and farming, especially of *kalo*. Today Hawaiian-language immersion schools integrate traditional food, farming, and related cultural practices into their curriculum, and students help restore ancient *loʻi* (taro fields) and clean fish ponds. Teachers are connecting with farmers who are growing traditional crops as well as food for local markets and schools, and their young people are getting out of the classroom and into the mud.

This kind of experiential learning is what Hawaiian teacher Makaluapua Kaʻawa says is the traditional *kino ike,* body knowledge—a hands-on (or, in the case of the taro patch, feet-first) way of reconnecting to the foods Hawaiians eat and the stories of their ancestors. Hawaiian language teacher Mehana Blaich says that the *loʻi kalo* is her favorite classroom, because it's where she teaches children the deeper meaning of food by telling the *kalo* story. "This is where we learn the most important lessons," she says, "because *kalo* teaches us who we are."

The work of "remembering" taro is being done by farmers. Taro expert Jerry Konanui is establishing a collection of the remaining eighty traditional varieties of taro on each of the islands.

Konanui and the taro farmers he works with say they don't need or want genetically engineered taro. "There is nothing wrong with taro," Konanui says. Some big growers and millers who are using chemicals are having problems, but the organic and traditional farmers aren't. "We're not losing taro varieties because of diseases and pests," says Konanui. "We are losing them because the taro industry is in monocrop mode and wants to grow super-taro." Konanui recites in detail how all the different varieties have different characteristics, flavors, names, and stories. It's that diversity, and traditional farming methods, he says, that are the best protection from drought and disease. "*Na kalo* is here. They're doing fine, just waiting for someone to plant them." Like all traditional farmers, he takes his cues from the plant. He says that if we grow it with care, it will keep its promise of productivity.

The Down-Turned Hand

While I was talking to Kawika Winter at Limahuli Garden about the challenges he faces in restoring the *ahupua'a* in Ha'ena, I asked him about the physical layout of the area. He stood up and went over to an aerial photograph of the Limahuli stream. It looked to me like a fern leaf, with fronds extending out from a central spine. No, Winter said, it's a hand. It's what they call "the down-turned hand." The name Limahuli means "turned hand." (*Lima* is "hand," *huli* is "to turn.") It refers to an old Hawaiian proverb that, roughly translated, says, "If your hand is turned up, you will be hungry; if your hand is turned toward the soil, your belly will be full."

The up-turned hand, Winter said, is not a positive symbol for Hawaiians. It is a sign of laziness or begging. The down-turned hand, however, represents the hard work of cultivating the land. It affirms traditional values of maintaining a harmonious relationship between the people, the land, and the sea. That's what his organization is doing here, he says, by restoring the forest, the *lo'i,* and the fish pond. Here, Native Hawaiians are integrating their work with the practices and philosophy of the *ahupua'a.* "My generation is building on what the ancestors started for us."

When pressed to say more about what this meant, Winter said he'd always understood what he needed to do by remembering that the land was his ancestor. Then he added that he relies on a proverb his grandfather taught him, repeating it in Hawaiian. It means, he explained, that in times of change, you have to be able to decide what to let go of and what to hang on to. Every generation faces this, he said. "We know that the way to get through difficult times is to use what was left to us—our land and our traditional knowledge. That will carry us into the future." He paused and then said, "This is our gift to the world."

Winter's work provides us all with the perfect model for local sustainability. And these ideas confirm the old adage many farmers use, which is that "everything you need is already right where you are." For Kaua'i, it's all right here—in the lay of the land, in the stories, and in the people. It's the perfect metaphor for the choices we all face: which way do we turn our hands, upward toward scarcity or downward toward the work of creating abundance?

A CABINET OF SEEDS DISPLAYED

These are the original monies of the earth,
In which invested, as the spark in fire,
They will produce a green wealth toppling tall,
A trick they do by dying, by decay,
In burial becoming each his kind
To rise in glory and be magnified
A million times above the obscure grave.

Reader, these samples are exhibited
For contemplation, locked in potency
And kept from act for reverence's sake.
May they remind us while we live on earth
That all economies are primitive;
And by their reservations may they teach
Our governors, who speak of husbandry
And think the hurricane, where power lies.

HOWARD NEMEROV

The Seeded Earth

The old warnings still have power to scare me:
Hubris comes to an ugly finish,
Irreverence is a greater oaf than Superstition.

W. H. AUDEN

The Garden of Eden

The story of the Garden of Eden is one of the most powerful stories ever told. All the children of Abraham—Christians, Muslims, and Jews—are taught the creation story in the biblical Book of Genesis. Its influence is unparalleled in the history of human life on earth. The way it's usually told is that in the beginning, there were seven days of creation. On the third day, the seeded earth was created. God said, "Let the earth bring forth grass, the herb that yields seed, and the fruit tree that yields fruit, according to its kind, whose seed is in itself, on the earth."

After all life on earth was created, Genesis says, the Creator then "planted a garden east of Eden" with every tree "good for food" and "pleasant to the sight." Two trees are specifically mentioned, the tree of the knowledge of good and evil and the tree of life. What happened next is well known. Adam and Eve ate the forbidden fruit from the tree of the knowledge of good and evil and were expelled from the garden.

But something else happens at that point in the story, something that is less well known but no less dramatic. In the Genesis story, Adam and Eve are given one simple rule: Do not eat the fruit of the tree of the knowledge of good and evil. When Adam and Eve fail their test, they are told that they are no longer entitled to life in Eden and that they will have to get their food through sweat and tears. They are expelled from the garden. This expulsion is often interpreted as punishment for their "original sin" of eating the forbidden fruit. But there is another explanation. When Adam and Eve are told to leave the garden, God says, "Behold, the man has become like one of Us, to know good and evil." What God says next, it seems to me, is the real reason they are expelled. God explains that Adam and Eve are no longer allowed in the garden "lest he put out his hand and take also of the tree of life, and eat, and live forever." Adam and Eve are sent away to prevent something from happening, something apparently even more important than eating from the tree of the knowledge of good and evil—touching the tree of life. This part of the Genesis story ends when, after Adam and Eve leave, God places the "cherubim at the east of the Garden of Eden, and a flaming sword which turned every way, to guard the way to the tree of life."

The powerful imagery in this story is an affirmation of the belief that all life is sacred. God evicted Adam and Eve from Eden and then put something as strong as the cherubim (angels) and something as vivid as a flaming, twirling sword in front of the tree of life to keep anyone from even approaching it. This obviously is meant to say that the tree of life is off-limits. The definition of the word "sacred" means something that's off-limits, set apart, to be treated with reverence.

For those who believe in the Bible, then, the Genesis creation story can be taken as an ancient and powerful admonition against reengineering the tree of life. The tree of life has been a symbol of fertility and abundance used by many cultures throughout the ages. Fifty years ago, when Watson and Crick suggested that DNA was the basis of life, they described its structure as a spiraling double helix, a graceful form that resembles a tree. And because of DNA's importance in replicating life, which is also the central metaphor of the tree, it's been suggested that DNA is in fact the tree of life. Therefore, severing DNA and reusing it to create new life, which is what recombinant DNA technology does, is "playing God," as it's often said. It could be used to enable us "to live forever."

The tree-of-life image has been used as a metaphor for evolution as well. The trunk of the tree is where life begins, in the cells that all living things share, and from there it grows more complex and becomes more intricate, forming the branches of the tree of evolution. Now, for the first time since life began, human activity—the combined impact of our technologies and environmental damage—is in itself altering the course of evolution. In *To Govern Evolution,* Walter Truett Anderson says that because of our actions, evolution no longer obeys the "remorseless logic of natural selection." He suggests that even if we think this is a good idea, we lack "the appropriate ethics and myths and political structures" to figure out how to manage this evolutionary governance. The Genesis story, however, read either literally or metaphorically, offers us a way to begin to develop those ethical structures.

I am retelling the biblical creation story because I want to underscore the importance of myths and creation stories in shaping how we think. Creation stories help us understand who we were in the past, and they help explain why we act the way we do now. They often contain some direction for our future as well. All creation stories reveal something about the underlying values of the people who tell them. Many creation stories have a number of core themes in common. One common theme, as we saw with the corn stories, is that human beings are given food as a gift from their Creator. That food isn't given in a stingy way, either; it's often provided with a profuse and abundant generosity, as in the Garden of Eden. Another common theme is that this magnificent gift comes with strings attached. A test or a temptation is dangled before the first people. If they fail that test, they face adverse consequences, often eerily reminiscent of our present condition.

Joseph Campbell's three-part "Historical Atlas of World Mythology" called *The Way of the Seeded Earth* tells many such stories. Like the Book of Genesis, these stories are often about whether or not people followed the rules or conditions that came with the gift of food. Invariably the prohibition that was given defined the responsibility of the human being toward the plant or animal. The "moral" of these stories was an affirmation of the need for a mutually respectful relationship between humans and the natural world. If that reciprocal covenant was broken, the result was hunger and scarcity.

The importance of the biblical creation story cannot be understated. It frames the way we think about technology, and it's usually read in a way that provides a religious justification for the human domination of nature. "We continually recycle this 'mandate from heaven' in the most important myths that shape our identity," says author Tom Hayden. Professor Carolyn Merchant goes further, saying that ever since "Adam and Eve tasted the fruit of the tree of the knowledge of good and evil," humanity has been "craving the knowledge of everything" and "using Christianity, science, technology, and capitalism in concert" to attain it.

Historian Lynn White Jr., who wrote "The Historical Roots of Our Ecologic Crisis" in 1967, was the first to point out how Judeo-Christian beliefs form the intellectual underpinnings of modern Western science and technology. He suggested that more technology, based as it is on these old beliefs, cannot possibly provide us with the answers we seek. His words echo what Einstein said about not being able to solve our problems with the same mentality that created them in the first place. White called for a rethinking of our relationship with nature. We'll have to "find a new religion, or rethink the old one," he said.

For the past forty years, the environmental movement has been struggling with ways to engage in this rethinking and resolve the moral questions raised by our environmental destruction. Environmental theologian Thomas Berry says that our moral dilemma is "all a question of story. We are in trouble just now because we do not have a good story. We are in between stories. The old story, the account of how the world came to be and how we fit into it, is no longer effective ... We need a new story." I agree.

Genetic engineering is severing our already frayed relationship with nature. A new mythology would help us reconnect and restore our reverence for life. How, then, do we go about finding the story, or stories, we need?

Good stories are always about the same thing: our quest for shared meaning and morality. The way to find good stories is just to do more storytelling. And as always, storytelling means both speaking and listening with an open mind. Unfortunately, we are losing the ability to do both. There is an urgent need to rescue storytelling from the clutches of the electronic media before we lose the art altogether. It needs to be infused with the intimacy of direct human interaction, so asking the people where you live to tell their stories might be the place to start. I have no idea how long this relearning might take, but I suspect it will be a while. We will have to keep practicing this long enough to learn how to talk to each other and embrace our differences. Then it will be a matter of gathering all these threads together and beginning to reweave a new context for our lives.

Retelling the Story of Agriculture

The story of agriculture used to be told as an epic struggle between people and nature. Ten thousand years into this narrative, it looks as if people have the upper hand. After all, food production is keeping up with population growth. And yet all this productivity comes at too high a cost to society and the environment. Industrial agriculture is laying waste to soil, water, forests, wildlife, biodiversity, the welfare of farm families, and the lifeways of traditional communities. Just as the chemical and genetic technologies of industrial agriculture appeared to have taken over in the twentieth century, a rebellion began to foment. Farmers and rural communities found alternative ways to farm that were organic, ecological, and traditional.

For the past sixty years, two very different visions for agriculture have continued to struggle over which one is best for both people and nature. As in any good drama, while the forces of good and evil have been having it out, something happened to raise the stakes. Lumbering onto center stage comes a twin-headed monster, the combined forces of global warming and species extinction, presenting us with the greatest threat to life on earth we have ever known. Suddenly the long-simmering conflict over how to feed ourselves shifts to the question of whether we will survive at all.

The story of agriculture, as told in industrialized societies, assumes that man is entitled to dominate nature. In that context, technologies that provide us with the mechanisms of control, like genetic engineering, make sense. The theme that "we have always fiddled with the genetics of plants" is part of industry's fanciful mythology. Industry likes to say that genetic engineering is no different from what farmers did thousands of years ago, but that's pure balderdash. It is true that people and plants have productively interacted for ages, but traditional plant breeding and recombinant DNA technology are not the same thing. Traditional plant breeding always respected the boundaries between species. Genetic engineering not only recombines species and creates new life forms, but it uses novel molecules that nature could never produce. Industry's story is an attempt to blur the differences between natural and artificial life forms. Two other assumptions about agriculture that appear in the standard story don't hold up, either. One is that we're smarter than people were in the past, and the other is that we're better off than they were.

The way the popular story usually goes is that someone spilled seeds and noticed that they grew, as if agriculture happened by accident. Most variations on the story begin in the Middle East. The general idea is that this is where the cultivation of grains and the domestication of animals began, reminiscent of the story of Cain and Abel. Then these ideas about how to produce food spread to the rest of the world. Anthropologist Brian Fagan says that this well-worn story, which is still widely told and believed, is nonsense. It "bears no resemblance to historical reality," he says. Using ancient texts, archaeology, archaeobiology, ethnobotany, anthropology, and genetics, Fagan and others have pieced together a very different explanation for how agriculture began.

The story that emerges is profoundly liberating. What actually happened is that between 8,000 and 12,000 years ago, very gradual changes took place in various parts of the world, largely in response to changes in climate. The story of agriculture turns out to be many stories. Agriculture arose independently all over the world, and in different cultural contexts. And it was a purposeful innovation. People selected a plant and worked with it. Over centuries, they adapted it to the needs of their lands and cultures. In Asia, it was rice. In South America, it was potatoes. In Mexico, it was corn. In the Middle East, it was wheat, barley, and peas. In other places, like Africa, Polynesia, India, and North America, people cultivated plants as staples, practicing a "protoagriculture" by nurturing the bulbs, grasses, and nuts they gathered. In each place there was a unique set of environmental and cultural conditions that gave rise to both the plants we now know as crops and the customs that formed around them.

The first person to map the relationship between crops and the places they began was the great Soviet biologist Nikolai Vavilov. In 1940, he identified seven distinct regions of the world where the most important domesticated plants were developed. He suggested that we call these places "centers of origin." So we know that agriculture arose independently in many different places on earth and that the shift from hunting and gathering to planting was gradual and intentional. These changes were based on a very close observation of natural systems over long periods of time. They were the result of accumulated wisdom, grounded in experience and perpetuated in the constant remembering of oral traditions. Not all human groups adopted agriculture. When they were able to do so, hunting-and-gathering societies maintained their preferred way of life well into modern times. However, in many places nomads and hunter-gatherers have been considered too "inefficient" in their use of land, so they have been and are being systematically eradicated.

We also know that industrial food production is not necessarily the optimal way to produce healthy food. Food systems that involve hunting, fishing, gathering, and cultivating the wild appear to take better care of the environment and provide a healthier diet with less effort and energy. In his essay "The Worst Mistake in the History of the Human Race," author Jared Diamond says that agriculture has actually contributed to the downfall of humanity and is the cause of slavery, poverty, famine, and most disease. Thus it's possible, even illuminating, to consider, or reconsider, retelling this whole story and rethinking our assumptions about agriculture. Our success as a species did not come about because we imposed our values on nature. As a survival strategy, domination is doomed. Recent studies have shown that cooperation is also a key survival strategy. Our outmoded engineering technologies require us to exert too much command and control over nature in an endless cycle of tyranny. Plus these technologies are too oversimplified to address the complexity of our most pressing ecological and social problems.

The human story is actually all about the emergence of a mutually productive relationship between people, plants, and place. The real story is about how, when we engaged in a cooperative reciprocal relationship, sustainability was achieved. The way to retell the story of agriculture, then, might be to begin with a reaffirmation of the basic covenant between ourselves and the seeded earth. Over the past several thousand years, we've engaged in mutually adaptive, interdependent, locally productive relationships. Domestication is useful, as long as it continues to be a dance we do with the plants and animals that want to work with us to maintain life. Genetic engineering has misled us into believing that we have to reformulate nature according to our own designs. Even if it works, it's a dead-end strategy, because it forces us to live within the extremely limited confines of the human imagination.

The new story, or stories, of agriculture would open up the possibility of reengaging in a more collaborative relationship with nature, based on the diversity and integrity of place. Then, when it comes time to solve the difficult problems we will inevitably face, we will have the experience and innovation we have gained as human communities to combine with our enlarged understanding of the ingenuity of the natural world. This way of thinking does require us to get comfortable with some level of uncertainty, because uncertainty is a necessary precondition for an open mind. Embracing uncertainty means rejecting the monotheism of molecular science, along with its enabling mythologies. It means resisting fundamentalist thinking of all kinds, in science, politics, and religion.

Stories help us navigate the mysteries and uncertainties of the world. That's where we keep the secrets of the human heart. If I were to pick someone as a guide on this perilous journey, it would be mythologist Joseph Campbell. His work underscores the transformational power of stories. He says that stories can heal our ecological wounds and bind us together in common values and purpose. And, not coincidentally, in *The Way of the Seeded Earth* he describes many ancient stories about the relationship between people, places, and plants. He does so geographically, in a pattern that matches Vavilov's map of the world's botanical centers of origin. Campbell doesn't refer to the centers of origin, but he does describe three different "matrices of agriculture," which he says originated in Southeast Asia, the Americas, and Africa. The stories he tells provide us with a rich mythological overlay for mapping the new story of agriculture, and they provide the key to finding the new stories we seek. They affirm the fact that our new stories must be as place-based and diverse as our communities.

Inspiration for these new stories can be found everywhere —in mythology, religion, art, traditional culture, literature, and even, or perhaps most especially, in science. Recent work in physics, for instance, confirms our intuitive understanding of the way the world works. Anyone who has planted a seed and watched a plant grow knows that life is a complex, emergent, and intelligent network of interactive forces. Now science validates that view. Stanford physicist Leonard Susskind, the father of string theory, says that physics and cosmology have now merged, leading us to a new way of thinking. Science, he explains, tells us about the world we know, cosmology helps us figure out what we might expect as life unfolds, and religion and mythology give meaning to it all. And, he says, we need all three.

The most remarkable thing Susskind says is that we now know that we don't inhabit a universe, we live in a "multiverse." Physics tells us that our existence has many dimensions. Our thinking and our storytelling need to catch up with that reality. Susskind, like physicist Fritjof Capra, is saying that our old simplistic and mechanistic ways of thinking are inadequate to the task at hand, which is understanding ourselves. The way forward for humanity is toward multidimensional thinking. We need stories that combine the rich inspiration of science, art, religion, and mythology to move us toward the "multiverse" of more socially tolerant, diverse, and complex locally adapted systems. They then will provide us with the moral compass we can use to evaluate what technologies are useful, for us and the rest of the natural world.

Campbell, who knew as much as anyone about the benefits of multidimensional thinking, used to talk about three stages of life. He said that the first is "living in the world," and it's all about survival, sex, and power. This, it seems to me, is where our science and twentieth-century technologies are stuck. The next stage is "coming into awareness." This involves discovering deep love and larger truths, like reverence for life. This is what the sustainability movement is all about and what it brings to the emerging "green" technologies. Campbell's third stage is "living in the sacred," where the illusion of separateness is finally lifted. After describing these stages, editor Diane Osbon brings them to life with one of Campbell's favorite references, attributed to an "old Apache storyteller," who tells us that "the plants, rocks, fire, water, are all alive. They watch us and see our needs. They see when we have nothing to protect us, and it is then that they reveal themselves and speak to us."

How will our story end? In tragedy? Or will there be an opportunity for transformation and resolution? No one alive today can know how it will all turn out. But every one of us has the opportunity to participate in its unfolding and to shape the outcome. And what better metaphor could we find to guide us than the seed? And just now, a remarkable seed has reemerged in a way and at a time that clearly reminds us of the power of the seed and the power of story. A 2,000-year-old date seed was found during archaeological excavations at Masada, a place of deep importance in Jewish history. It was brought back to life by an American botanist working in Israel and is now a small tree. It's called the Methuselah seed. It could reestablish the ancient dates that fed the people of Judea at the time of Christ. And as a palm tree, it returns to us an ancient symbol of peace.

Seeds are messengers from the past. They are an embodiment of hope for the future. Seeds are a promise of life to come. They endure because they are generous. They survive by being resilient, abundant, and adaptable. The story of seeds is also our story. We can be guided by the way of the seed and by knowing that what we do to seeds, we do to ourselves. One thing is certain: the future of seeds is in our hands.

ACKNOWLEDGMENTS

It's amazing how many people it takes to write a book. For all the help and inspiration I've been given, I am deeply grateful.

This book would not have been possible without two people in particular. Thanks to Ed Ayres, editor emeritus of *World Watch Magazine*, for his counsel and mentoring. And just when I needed it most, Nancy Schuab came through with kindness and generosity and provided me with a place to finish the book at Tunitas Creek Ranch.

Thanks to Ignacio Chapela for his friendship and remarkable insight into the invisible world. The women in my writers' group are the best; thanks for all the help, cookies, and laughs. Special thanks to Melissa Nelson, whose work with the Cultural Conservancy is close to my heart and whose friendship I treasure. Thanks to Lisa Hamilton for being so very smart and sensible and to Chera Van Burg for her keen insights. Other writers have been my guardian angels, including Chellis Glendinning, who was there from the very beginning. Thanks also to Anne Lamott, who always says the right thing, and to China Galland. And thanks to Mark Dowie for great advice over the years. Thanks very much to Peter Barnes and Mesa Refuge for getting me started, and thanks to my editor at Beacon, Brian Halley, for his vision.

To all those who contributed information or took the time to be interviewed or to comment on the text, thank you so much, especially Nazreen Kadir, Pat Mooney, Hope Shand, Chuck Benbrook, Bill Freese, Kawika Winter, Miguel Santistevan, Percy Schmeiser, Bryce Lundberg, J.J. Haapala, Richard Strohman, Beth Burrows, Joe Mendelson, Martha Crouch, Ross Gelbspan, Henry Shands, Dave Ellis, Chris Kobayashi, and Gary Nabhan. Dan McGuire, thanks for all the great resources on corn. A special thanks to Mark Ritchie and to Vo-Tong Xuan. And a deep bow to those who are constant sources of inspiration: Wendell Berry, Wes Jackson, Al Krebs, Angus Wright, Paul Hawken, Michael Pollan, Wendy Johnson, and especially Nina Simons, Kenny Ausubel, the Bioneers, Code Pink, and all you Unreasonable Women. Thanks to Bokara Legendre for her Bioneers presentation on cosmology. I will always be indebted to the incredible Caroline Casey for her considerable genius and irreverent wisdom.

Thanks to everyone at KPFA and especially Weyland Southon for believing in the power of radio and my place on the air. Thanks to Jon Fromer and Belva Davis at KQED and to Susan Clark at the Columbia Foundation for her remarkable work, and to all those I've worked with at Food First, Community Alliance with Family Farmers, Earth Island, and the Center for Ecoliteracy; they have contributed to this book more than they know. Thanks to reporters Fred Pearce and Andy Meek for their help.

For strengthening my love and knowledge of Hawai'i, *mahalo nui loa* to J. Kalani English, Mililani Trask, and especially Mahealani Cypher, for her long-time *aloha 'aina*. *Mahalo* to all the native leaders, farmers, and activists working for a sustainable GMO-free Hawai'i, especially Nancy Redfeather and Jeri DiPietro. On O'ahu, thanks to Cha Smith and Coleen Kelly, for so much, and to Mary Lacques, who's the best. *Mahalo* to Carla Crow and Mickael Om Mast for their hospitality on Maui. Finally, thank you to Koohan Paik, for being the most astute observer of the world I know, a great writer and friend.

There is someone who is in a category all his own: Dick Pervier. Every Friday for the past ten years, Dick has phoned a few fortunate friends and read them a poem. His readings have inspired the poetry in this book, and in my heart.

Where would I be without the love and support of my family? They have been wonderful. Thanks especially to my children, Michael Rowan, Sara Desmond, and Emily Rowan. While doing this work I have missed you and your children, Nathan, Rowan, Lily, and Henry. While I worked, the screensaver on my computer would display photographs of their smiling faces in their homes and gardens and on our travels together, and they kept me going. I hope they know I wrote this book for them and for their children.

Thanks to Naomi Hoffman for being such a loving sister. For a keen love of plants, I have to thank my mom and my sister Maryhope. For her constant protection and healing wisdom, I thank Grams, Florence Jones, the late top doctor of the Winnemem Wintu tribe. And last, thanks to the one person who has made it all possible, my husband, Richard McCombs.

SOURCES AND RESOURCES

This book is based on my own investigative work as a journalist, my twelve years of research and reporting on agriculture and genetic engineering, and hundreds of interviews, publications, organizations, and websites. Listed below by chapter, in the order they are first mentioned, are some of these resources. Where the source is cited in the text or the information can be easily found using an Internet search engine, it is not listed here.

Preface

Quotations from Watson's speech were taken from the author's audio recording.

Wright, Susan. *Molecular Politics: Developing American and British Regulatory Policy for Genetic Engineering, 1972–1982.* Chicago: University of Chicago Press, 1994.

Introduction

Information on the Arctic seed vault, including construction photographs, can be found at the Global Crop Diversity Trust website: www.croptrust.org.

One: Trade Secrets

Dora Jane Hamblin's "Has the Garden of Eden Been Located at Last?" appeared in *Smithsonian Magazine* 18, no. 2 (May 1987).

Fred Pearce's "Returning War-Torn Farmland to Productivity" appeared in *New Scientist,* January 22, 2005.

Further information on Order 81 and international issues related to genetic engineering is available from Genetic Resources Action International (GRAIN), a nongovernmental organization devoted to agricultural biodiversity based on people's control over genetic resources and local knowledge: www.grain.org.

More information on the work of the Consultative Group on International Agricultural Research (CGIAR) and its publication *Healing Wounds: How the International Research Centers of the CGIAR Help Restore Agriculture in Countries Affected by Conflicts and Natural Disasters* is available at www.cgiar.org. Links to all of its publications and centers, including ICARDA, can also be found at this website.

Fowler, Cary, and Pat Mooney. *Shattering: Food, Politics, and the Loss of Genetic Diversity.* Tucson: University of Arizona Press, 1990.

Kay, Lily E. *The Molecular Vision of Life: Caltech, The Rockefeller Foundation, and the Rise of the New Biology.* New York: Oxford University Press, 1993.

Shaw, Bernard. *The Intelligent Woman's Guide to Socialism and Capitalism.* New York: Brentano's, 1928.

Further information on the regulation of genetically engineered foods can be found at the Center for Food Safety's website, www.centerforfoodsafety.org; the Genetic Engineering Policy Alliance's website, www.geopolicyalliance.org; and the Pew Initiative on Food and Biotechnology's website, www.pewagbiotech.org.

Ho, Mae-Wan. *Living with the Fluid Genome.* London: Institute of Science in Society, 2003.

Myers, Nancy, and Carol Raffensperger, eds. *Precautionary Tools for Reshaping Environmental Policy.* Cambridge, MA: MIT Press, 2006.

Two: Trespass

Chargaff, Edwin. *Heraclitean Fire: Sketches from a Life before Nature.* New York: Rockefeller University Press, 1978.

Union of Concerned Scientists publications are available at www.ucsusa.org.

Further information on agricultural genetic engineering and contamination issues can be found at the Organic Consumers Association's website, www.organicconsumers.org, and for Hawai'i at GMO Free Hawaii's website, www.higean.org, which has links to websites for each island.

Jeffrey M. Smith's books are *Seeds of Deception: Exposing Industry and Government Lies About the Safety of the Genetically Engineered Foods You're Eating* (White River Junction, VT: Yes! Books, 2003) and *Genetic Roulette: The Documented Health Risks of Genetically Engineered Foods* (White River Junction, VT: Yes! Books, 2007).

Joy Bergelson's "Promiscuity in Transgenic Plants" appeared in *Nature* 395 (September 1998).

"Hawaii's Seed Industry Plants to Grow in Acreage and Employees" appeared in *Pacific Business News,* Honolulu, October 14, 2005.

"Technology Jobs Down Despite Tax Credit" appeared in *West Hawai'i Today,* October 7, 2006.

More information about the role of pesticides in GMO agriculture in general and the herbicide Roundup in particular can be found at Pesticide Action Network's website, www.panna.org. Its publication "Rethinking Roundup" is available at www.panna.org/resources/panups/panup_20050805.dv.html, and a collection of studies on Roundup is available at www.mindfully.org/Pesticide/Monsanto-Roundup-Glyphosate.htm.

Three: Political Science

Michigan State University published its study of the Novartis/UCB agreement, *External Review of the Collaborative Research Agree-*

ment Between Novartis Agricultural Discovery Institute, Inc. and The Regents of the University of California, in July 2004.

Soley, Lawrence C. *Leasing the Ivory Tower: The Corporate Takeover of Academia.* Cambridge, MA: South End Press, 1995.

Sara Rimer's "A Caution Against Mixing Commerce and Academics" appeared in the *New York Times,* April 16, 2003.

Allison Wilson, Jonathan Latham, and Ricarda Steinbrecher's "Genome Scrambling—Myth or Reality? Transformation-Induced Mutations in Transgenic Crop Plants" is available at www.econexus.info.

Richard Lewontin is the author of *The Triple Helix: Gene, Organism, and Environment* (Cambridge, MA: Harvard University Press, 2000), and his "The DNA Era: Cellular Complexity and the Failures of Genetic Engineering" appeared in *GeneWatch Magazine,* August 2003.

Hans-Hinrich Kaatz's study of bees was cited in "GM Genes 'Jump Species Barrier,'" *Guardian Weekly* (London), May 2000.

Michael K. Hansen's "Genetic Engineering Is Not an Extension of Conventional Plant Breeding," an unpublished paper, and the work of Chuck Benbrook and other papers cited in this chapter can be found online at Benbrook's former information clearinghouse, www.biotech-info.net.

D. Quist and I. Chapela's "Transgenic DNA Introgressed into Traditional Maize Landraces in Oaxaca, Mexico" appeared in *Nature* 414 (November 29, 2001).

Four: The Ownership Society

Kimbrell, Andrew, and Joseph Mendelson. *Monsanto vs. U.S. Farmers.* Washington, DC: Center for Food Safety, 2004.

"Saving Seeds Subjects Farmers to Suits Over Patent" appeared in the *New York Times,* November 2, 2003.

"The Idea Economy" appeared in the *International Herald Tribune,* October 2005.

More information about the critique of intellectual property rights and the commons can be found at the Creative Commons website, www.creativecommons.org, and at www.onthecommons.org, a site sponsored by the Tomales Bay Institute.

More information about terminator technologies can be found at the ETC Group website, www.etcgroup.org.

Five: Who Owns Rice?

Hargrove, Thomas R. *A Dragon Lives Forever: War and Rice in Vietnam's Mekong Delta 1969–1991, and Beyond.* New York: Ivy Books/Ballantine, 1994.

The International Rice Research Center website is www.irri.org.

The ETC report mentioned is entitled *Global Seed Industry Concentration,* from the ETC Group Communique, Issue #90, September/October 2005.

Resources on hunger can be found at the Institute for Food and Development Policy's website, www.foodfirst.org, and the United Nation's Food and Agriculture Organization website, www.fao.org.

Six: The Botany of Scarcity

Pearce, Fred. *With Speed and Violence: Why Scientists Fear Tipping Points in Climate Change.* Boston: Beacon Press, 2007.

Speth, James Gustave. *Red Sky at Morning: America and the Crisis of the Global Environment.* New Haven, CT: Yale University Press, 2004.

Pimm, Stuart L. *A Scientist Audits the Earth.* Piscataway, NJ: Rutgers University Press, 2001.

Rosenzweig, Cynthia. *Climate Change and U.S. Agriculture: The Impacts of Warming and Extreme Weather Events on Productivity, Plant Diseases, and Pests.* Boston, MA: Center for Health and the Global Environment, Harvard Medical School, 2000. More information on the impacts of global warming on agriculture can be found in studies done by Cynthia Rosenzweig and Daniel Hillel, such as

"Potential Impacts of Climate Change on Agriculture and Food Supply," published in *Consequences* in 1995 and found online at www.gcrio.org/CONSEQUENCES/summer95/agriculture.html.

Henry Fountain's "Global Warming on the Forest Floor" appeared in the *New York Times,* October 3, 2006.

More information on agriculture and climate change is available from the Worldwatch Institute and in Worldwatch publications at www.worldwatch.org.

Seven: The Botany of Abundance

Kloppenburg, Jack. *First the Seed: The Political Economy of Plant Biotechnology.* 2d ed. Madison: University of Wisconsin Press, 2004.

Doyle, Jack. *Altered Harvest: Agriculture, Genetics, and the Fate of the World's Food Supply.* New York: Viking, 1985.

Hawken, Paul. *Blessed Unrest: How the Largest Movement in the World Came into Being and Why No One Saw It Coming.* New York: Viking, 2007.

Jackson, Wes. *New Roots for Agriculture.* New ed. Lincoln: University of Nebraska Press, 1985. Jackson's writing and the research of the Land Institute are available at www.landinstitute.org.

Benyus, Janine. *Biomimicry: Innovation Inspired by Nature.* New York: Morrow, 1997.

Eight: Ripe for Change

Wendell Berry's "Renewing Husbandry" appeared in *Orion,* September/October 2005.

Schlosser, Eric. *Fast Food Nation: The Dark Side of the All-American Meal.* Boston: Houghton Mifflin, 2001.

Michael Pollan's book *The Omnivore's Dilemma: A Natural History of Four Meals* (New York: Penguin, 2006) as well as his other writings are available at www.michaelpollan.com.

Marion Nestle's books include *Food Politics: How the Food Industry Influences Nutrition and Health* (Berkeley: University of California

Press, 2002) and *Safe Food: Bacteria, Biotechnology, and Bioterrorism* (Berkeley: University of California Press, 2003).

Imhoff, Daniel. *Food Fight.* Healdsburg, CA: Watershed Media, 2007.

Anderson, M. Kat. *Tending the Wild: Native American Knowledge of the Management of California's Natural Resources.* Berkeley: University of California Press, 2005.

Nine: A Conversation with Corn

Visser, Margaret. *Much Depends on Dinner: The Extraordinary History and Mythology, Allure and Obsessions, Perils and Taboos of an Ordinary Meal.* New York: Grove, 1986.

Gonzalez, Roberto. *Zapotec Science: Farming and Food in the Northern Sierra of Oaxaca.* Austin: University of Texas Press, 2001.

Charles Mann's "1491, America Before Columbus" appeared in the *Atlantic Monthly,* March 2002.

Fussell, Betty. *The Story of Corn.* New York: Knopf, 1992.

Waters, Frank. *The Book of the Hopi.* New York: Viking, 1963.

Ten: The Down-Turned Hand

LaDuke, Winona. *Recovering the Sacred: The Power of Naming and Claiming.* Cambridge, MA: South End Press, 2005.

Epilogue

Teitel, Martin, and Kimberly Wilson. *Genetically Engineered Food: Changing the Nature of Nature.* Rochester, VT: Park Street Press, 1999.

Merchant, Carolyn. *Reinventing Eden: The Fate of Nature in Western Culture.* New York: Routledge, 2003.

Campbell, Joseph. *Historical Atlas of World Mythology: Volume II, The Way of the Seeded Earth, Parts One, Two, and Three.* New York: Perennial, 1989.

Osbon, Diane K. *A Joseph Campbell Companion: Reflections on the Art of Living.* New York: HarperCollins, 1991.

Berry, Thomas. *The Dream of the Earth.* San Francisco: Sierra Club Books, 1988.

Additional Sources

The following books also provided inspiration and information:

Anderson, Edgar. *Plants, Man & Life.* Berkeley: University of California Press, 1952.

Bailey, Britt, and Lappé, Marc. *Engineering the Farm: Ethical and Social Aspects of Agricultural Biotechnology* (Washington, DC: Island Press, 2002) and *Against the Grain: Biotechnology and the Corporate Takeover of Your Food* (Monroe, ME: Common Courage Press, 1998).

Berry, Wendell. *Life Is a Miracle: An Essay Against Modern Superstition.* New York: Counterpoint, 2000.

Brown, Lester R. *Plan B 2.0: Rescuing a Planet Under Stress and a Civilization in Trouble.* Washington, DC: Earth Policy Institute, 2006.

Gelbspan, Ross. *The Heat Is On* (Boston: Addison-Wesley, 1997) and *Boiling Point* (New York: Basic Books, 2004).

Goodenough, Ursula. *The Sacred Depths of Nature.* New York: Oxford University Press, 1998.

Hart, Kathleen. *Eating in the Dark: America's Experiment with Genetically Engineered Food.* New York: Pantheon, 2002.

Ho, Mae-Wan. *Genetic Engineering: Dream or Nightmare?* London: Gill & Macmillan, 1999.

Juma, Calestous. *The Gene Hunters: Biotechnology and the Scramble for Seeds.* Princeton, NJ: Princeton University Press, 1989.

Nabhan, Gary. *Enduring Seeds: Native American Agriculture and Wild Plant Conservation.* New York: North Point, 1989.

Pavord, Anna. *The Naming of Names: The Search for Order in the World of Plants.* New York: Bloomsbury, 2005.

Raeburn, Paul. *The Last Harvest: The Genetic Gamble That Threatens to Destroy American Agriculture.* New York: Simon & Schuster, 1995.

Raven, Peter, et al., eds. *Biology of Plants.* 5th ed. New York: Worth, 1992.

Wright, Angus. *The Death of Ramon Gonzalez: The Modern Agricultural Dilemma.* Austin: University of Texas Press, 1990, rev. 2005.

Wright, Ronald. *A Short History of Progress.* New York: Carroll & Graf, 2004.

INDEX

academics. *See* research institutions
Achitoff, Paul, 38
Adolphe, Dan, 36
AgBioWorld, 60
Agricultural Research Source (ARS), 136–37
agriculture: climate change and, 121–27; culture in, 158–62; economy and, 20–21, 65–66, 133; genetic engineering and, xvi–xix, 8; in Iraq, 3–6; labor in, 104–5, 190–91; story of, xviii–xix, 199–205; in United States, 6–8, 65–66, 150, 168–74; in Vietnam, 87–91, 104–5. *See also* industrial agriculture; sustainable agriculture
Agrobacterium, 53–54
ahupua'a, 183–84, 190–91
Alegria, Rafael, 156

alfalfa, 34
Altered Harvest (Doyle), 133
American Corn Growers Association, 38
American Farm Bureau, 27
American Seed Trade Association (ASTA), 132
Amstutz, Dan, 5
Anderson, M. Kat, 158
Anderson, Walter Truett, 197
Animal and Plant Health Inspection Service (APHIS), 12–13
animal feed: cultural decline and, 175; GMOs in, 17, 27, 41; in industrial agriculture, 66, 129, 173; land use and, 120; in sustainable agriculture, 141, 154
antibiotic resistance markers, 15, 39
antibiotics, 39, 78, 79, 173
Asgrow Seed Company, 74
AstraZeneca, 100